MW00335004

Motivational Numerology

And How Numbers Affect Your Life

Introducing The Wizard's Star

SALLY FAUBION

Seven Locks Press

Santa Ana, California
Minneapolis, Minnesota
Washington, D.C.

© 2001 by Sally Faubion. All rights reserved.

No part of this publication may be reproduced, distributed, or transmitted in any form or by any means, including photocopying, recording, or other electronic or mechanical methods, or by any information storage and retrieval system, without prior written permission from the publisher, except for brief quotations embodied in critical reviews and certain other noncommercial uses permitted by copyright law. For permission requests, write to the publisher, addressed "Attention: Permissions Coordinator," at the address below.

Seven Locks Press
P.O. Box 25689
Santa Ana, CA 92799
(800) 354-5348

Individual Sales. This book is available through most bookstores or can be ordered directly from Seven Locks Press at the address above.

Quantity Sales. Special discounts are available on quantity purchases by corporations, associations, and others. For details, contact the "Special Sales Department" at the publisher's address above.

Printed in the United States of America

Library of Congress Cataloging-in-Publication Data
Faubion, Sally, 1944–
    Motivational numerology: and how numbers affect your life: introducing wizard's star / Sally Faubion
        p. cm.
ISBN 0-929765-97-4
    1. Numerology. I. Title

Cover and Interior Design by Sparrow Advertising & Design
Graphic design of Wizard's Star by Bonnie Spence

The author and publisher assume neither liability nor responsibility to any person or entity with respect to any direct or indirect loss or damage caused, or alleged to be caused, by the information contained herein, or for errors, omissions, inaccuracies, or any other inconsistency within these pages, or for unintentional slights against people or organizations.

Motivational Numerology

And How Numbers Affect Your Life

Dear Marilyn,
as I said in our reading, you are a blessing to this earth plane. Thank you for your presence and your high knowledge.

Love,
Jackson
8/03

This book is dedicated to
Don Vidal whose incredible
encouragement and immeasurable support
helped to make this book possible.

Table of Contents

Preface

I began studying the science of numerology at the age of 20 and considered it a hobby for about ten years. Gradually it began to consume most of my spare time and even some of my working hours. Over the following twenty years, I became virtually obsessed and possessed by its study and application and amazed by its accuracy.

I owned a service business in downtown San Francisco throughout my 20s and 30s and hired most of my employees by using my knowledge of numerology. Analyzing all my family members and friends became a passion. Practically every person who crossed my path, as well as everyone who gained any public notoriety (whose birth dates and names were attainable), got analyzed. It seemed the more I used numerology, the better I was able to decipher personality characteristics of people I knew only casually and even some I had never met before. I gained knowledge into their pasts and present, and found I was also able to forecast their future.

Thirty years later I am still awe-struck by the interpretations and understanding I derive from numerology, and I believe it is a tool that has helped me to develop my psychic abilities.

Today I use my expertise and knowledge of numerology as my main source of income. I give corporate, convention, and spa lectures; perform at parties, appear on T.V. and the radio, write articles for national magazines, and consult for individuals as well as businesses. I have also produced two successful lines of greeting cards, a calendar, two board games, and other books on the subject of numerology as well as other metaphysical topics. In short, I am fortunate enough to be living an American dream—that of making a living by working at my favorite hobby!

Introduction

After reading more than one hundred books on the subject of numerology, I discovered that most authors/numerologists have their own unique points of view. Many, in fact, introduce totally new concepts that seem to be their own concoction. Moreover, there is little consistency from one practitioner to the next with regard to the terms used to describe the numbers in a numerological chart. For example, depending on which numerology book you happen to be reading, you will find the number I call the Destiny number referred to as the "fate number," the "birth path," the "birth force," or the "life force."

I began my study with the Pythagorean philosophy (Pythagoras, the Greek mathematician and philosopher, was the father of numerology in the western world), which assigns the numbers 1 through 9 to the letters in the Roman alphabet. There are also the Chaldean and ancient Hebrew, the Rosecrusian philosophies, and the Jewish Kabalah, along with other, more obscure ancient and modern concepts. Although I have worked with all these methods to one extent or another, the Pythagorean philosophy seemed to pluck hardest at some chord of understanding in my being. It is my opinion, however, that if you're a serious student of the science, it's good to learn and apply all the different philosophies to ensure that you are using the one that seems to resonate with you.

Motivational Numerology is based primarily on the Pythagorean theory of numerology, but I have woven in some aspects from the other philosophies as well. Since I have refined this approach during the three decades of my practice, I can attest that it works! For the purpose of this book, my goal was to simplify the concepts so that the reader may easily and quickly learn the basics of numerology.

After giving thousands of numerology readings over the years, I found it very helpful to offer my clients visual images of the numbers that related to their life so that they might "see" more clearly how each of the six basic numbers in a numerology chart apply to their character, personality, and surroundings.

Although I have used different imagery objects over the years, Pythagoras' five-pointed star called "The Wizard's Foot" (formed by three even-sided triangles) was so well-suited to the purposes of this book, that it has become the cornerstone of my readings today. Having added my own interpretation and colors to The Wizard's Foot, I have chosen to call it "The Wizard's Star" and use it as the primary tool for helping my readers to envision and understand their unique personality compositions.

Another helpful imagery exercise that I have used to learn more about the numbers is to study the number definitions and characteristics as they correlate with famous people's birth dates and name numbers. Numerous famous people's birth dates and names are supplied as examples in the back of this book.

Over time, as you learn to apply numerology in your life, you'll find your psychic powers growing. You'll instinctively understand more and more about yourself and other people, and you should begin to make wiser choices even without referring to the book. It is my hope that as you learn and apply the tenets in this book, you will begin an exciting journey toward greater personal insight and power!

Last, but certainly not least, I want to thank Roxanne Cameron for her astute style, fine editing work, and encouragement; and Bonnie Spence for helping with the design of the Wizard's Star and for her gracious and effective networking, without which the birth of this book may not have occurred. I also want to thank my nephew, Sushuma, for his insightful counsel and exceptional website design which includes the Wizard's Star and the compatibility charts.

Sally Faubion
San Francisco, California
March 2001

Chapter 1

Numbers, The Alphabet, Pythagoras, and Numerology

Society inundates us with numbers, not only during our school years and in business, but also in our daily lives. Think about all the numbers in your life: Social Security, driver's license, credit cards, bank accounts, computer codes, ATM code, your address and phone number, to say nothing of constantly consulting your watch, clocks, calendars, and your computer. If you believe you have a lucky number or observe recurring numbers in your life, those feelings and insights may not be a coincidence. To say numbers play a significant role in our lives is definitely an understatement. Mankind is coming to a point where numbers continue to play an ever-increasing part in our lives and futures.

The following brief accounts of the evolution of numbers, counting, and the alphabet reveal their very important beginnings.

THE BIRTH OF NUMBERS AND COUNTING

It is impossible to know when man began to develop numbers and counting, but anthropologists have found some form of counting present in the most primitive cultures. The oldest numeration method has been traced to the Paleolithic era in the form of notches incised in reindeer antlers, dating back more than thirty thousand years. Wood and stones were also found to have been used in ancient times as counting devices, along with peoples' body parts. The latter was a complex corporal numerical system that assigned a number to each body part and position. This method included not only the use of the fingers as numerical digits, but also the ears, arms, legs, torso, head, and individual finger joints and knuckles.

It is a known fact today that ten digits alone can represent all the numbers in the world, and isn't it interesting that the human body has ten fingers and ten toes. This body-part method is called "digital calculation," and it is still in use today in some African countries.

Various forms of numeration were used by the Egyptians, Greeks, and Chinese. The Mayan and Inca Indians also had as many as four very sophisticated and unrelated methods that they used; and the Aztecs, Ethiopians, Hebrews, and Romans had their own versions, too.

Interesting and inventive devices used for numeration and calculation purposes in ancient times included the use of a *quipu*, knotted ropes attached to a cord, used by the Incas; molded clay stones known as *calculi* used by the ancient Sumerians; Egyptian hieroglyphs, pebbles, pearls, shells, and sticks, and carrying small bags of flour which, when spilled on a floor or table, could then be used to trace digits on the surface. Other inspired gadgets were large stone tablets coated with wax that could be rubbed clean and reused (the first chalkboards), and the table abacus, called the "computing table" (which can be traced as far back as 400 BC). The ingenious and useful invention of paper by the Chinese in the 2nd century AD, finally gave man the capability of recording his calculations for future reference.

The digits 1 through 9 were invented by the Indians in the 3rd century BC and positional numeration (the zero giving value to each number position) was also invented in India in the 5th century AD. This form of calculation was revolutionary in those times, and word began to spread about its advantages. It found its way to the east via an Indian ambassador who went to Baghdad and taught it to the Arabs. Al-Kharizini, the great Arab mathematician, later transported it to Europe. The western world still gives credit to the Arabs for numerals, but modern-day Arabs rightly give this credit to the Indians. Europeans even honored Al-Kharizini by referring to numbers as Arabic numerals, a description that has held into modern times. A version of those Arabic numerals is still in use in Europe and the Americas today.

Modern man appears to have taken numbers to a monumental level of importance. Consider, for example, the foreboding news coverage in 1999 about the possibility of a worldwide catastrophe should the vast network of computers around the world not change from 1999 to 2000. Although the millennium transition went without a hitch, it is obvious that numbers can be powerful. In that vein, it is especially interesting that, in numerology, numbers also have personalities, which you will learn about later in this book.

THE EVOLUTION OF THE ROMAN ALPHABET

The modern Roman alphabet had a long and interesting journey to its present-day letters and their appearance. Its roots stem from the ancient Hebrew alphabet of 22 letters. In those ancient times, only the privileged, usually rabbis, were allowed to decipher and use the alphabet. And, just in case it were to fall in the hands of someone of the lower echelons, this first alphabet did not include vowels; and, as a consequence, no one except the rabbis could understand written composition. Even today, scholars of the complicated Hebrew numeric system (called the kabala) find certain aspects of the Hebrew alphabet to be a mystery.

The next link in our alphabet's evolution was made by the Phoenicians who adopted their alphabet from the ancient Hebrews, although they made significant changes to it. Soon thereafter, the Greeks borrowed from the Phoenicians to form their own alphabet. The Greek alphabet was passed on to the Etruscans, who devised their own version that was later translated into Latin. Finally, it was this Latin version which ultimately lead to the formation of the Roman alphabet in approximately 600 BC.

The modern Roman alphabet was formulated between the 3rd century AD and the invention of printing in the 15th century AD.

PYTHAGORAS AND NUMEROLOGY

Numerology is an ancient metaphysical science based on symbols and cycles. This "science of numbers" can be traced back more than five thousand years. In fact, the archives of the ancient Chaldeans of Babylonia and the Phoenicians contain forms of numerology that were used by those cultures for trading and communication purposes.

Numerology was introduced to the western world by Pythagoras, the Greek mathematician and philosopher who lived around 500 BC. Anyone who has taken a geometry class will recall that it was Pythagoras who propounded the theory of the isosceles triangle. (The diameter of the square on the right angle of an isosceles triangle is equal to the sum of the diameters of the squares on the other two sides, or $A^2 + B^2 = C^2$.) And, it was Pythagoras who presented the concept that "all things in the universe can be reduced to a number" and that "all numbers resonate the profound forces of the universe," namely, energy forces.

Pythagoras spent thirty years traveling throughout the eastern cultures collecting knowledge of the ancient occult traditions. In Egypt, he studied the Oracle of the Delphi and the mysteries of the Isis. He also received special instruction in Persia by the Zoroasters about the doctrines of the Magi. In Babylonia, he learned about the "Science of Number" from the Chaldeans, and he also journeyed to India where he gathered knowledge from the Brahman priests about the sacred tenets of the Hindu Vedas. On yet another leg of his travels, he explored the secret traditions of the kabala from Hebrew rabbis. Various aspects of each of those ancient doctrines were used by Pythagoras to render numerology (a word he coined). Some of those ancient sciences are still in use today, namely the Science of Number by the Chaldeans and the Jewish kabala. However, Pythagorean numerology continues to be the most accepted method used by modern-day numerologists.

Chapter 2
Numbers and Letters: How They Add Up

When you see a numerologist quickly cover a page with letters, numbers, and sums, it looks more complicated than it is. The only arithmetic you need to know is plain old addition. It's absolutely not necessary for you to be a "numbers person" to practice basic numerology. Unlike astrology, you don't need a complicated star chart or any other aids.

There are just two rules you need to remember if you want to do simple numerology yourself.

RULE ONE

When you add up the numbers in your birth date or the number equivalents in the letters of your name, you almost always need to reduce these numbers to a single digit. (The "almost" implies that there are exceptions, and there are. They will be explained later under Master Numbers.)

Here's an example of how numerology math is done:

Suppose your birth date is August 20, 1982. First you add 8 (August is the 8th month) to 20 to 1982, as follows:

$$\begin{array}{r} 8 \\ 20 \\ \underline{1982} \\ \text{Total} = \ 2010 \end{array}$$

That's four digits, and you need to reduce them to one. So you next add these digits together: $2 + 0 + 1 + 0$. The total is 21. You still don't have one digit. So you add the digits together again: $2 + 1 = 3$. Your full birth date is a 3. What does this mean? You'll see in a later chapter.

You'll get the same result, incidentally, if you add all the numbers across $(8 + 2 + 0 + 1 + 9 + 8 + 2 = 30$ and $3+0 = 3)$. Do your addition whichever way is easiest for you, and use the other method to check your figures. You can always use a calculator, of course, but you might agree that it is good to exercise your brain with a little math every once in a while.

Master Numbers: The numbers 11 and 22 are called Master numbers in numerology. You will learn more about them later in the book. If your birth date or name numbers reduce to either of these two numbers, regardless of which addition process you use, do not reduce them to a single digit.

Example: Birth date of August 14, 1962:

$$8$$
$$14$$
$$\underline{1962}$$

Total   1984   and $1 + 9 + 8 + 4 = 22$

Using the "string" method with the birth date of October 29, 1970:

$1 + 0 + 2 + 9 + 1 + 9 + 7 + 0 = 29$ and $2 + 9 = 11$

RULE TWO

Your name and your birth date contain all the information you need to complete your numerological profile. Your birth date is a number (e.g., 12/6/71), and your name is a number.

How is your name—composed of letters—a number? Each letter of the alphabet has its numerical equivalent. See the diagram below:

1	2	3	4	5	6	7	8	9
A	B	C	D	E	F	G	H	I
J	K	L	M	N	O	P	Q	R
S	T	U	V	W	X	Y	Z	

As you see, A, J, and S all have the value of 1. B, K, and T all have the value of 2, and so forth. In Chapter 5 you will learn how to separate the numbers in your name to extract the Character, Soul Urge, and Hidden Agenda numbers.

THE SIX NUMBERS DERIVED FROM YOUR BIRTH DATE AND NAME AND THEIR SIGNIFICANCE

There are three different numbers derived from your birth date—the Destiny, the Personality, and the Attitude. There are also three numbers that are derived from you name—the Character, the Soul Urge, and the Hidden Agenda. The following explanations for these numbers are presented to clarify the importance of each of them as they relate to your personality and numerology chart.

THE THREE NUMBERS DERIVED FROM THE BIRTH DATE:

1. The Destiny number: This number is found by adding all the numbers in your date of birth together and reducing them to a single digit. As the word Destiny implies, it represents what you came into this life to accomplish, what careers are best suited to you, how you like your surroundings, who you gravitate toward and retain as friends and mates, and what activities or social atmosphere you most desire. It is the "what" you came to achieve and get out of this life.

2. The Personality number: This number is derived from the day of the month you were born. This number is representative of your "inside" personality. It influences the personality you exhibit to those who are closest to you—your family members and intimate friends. It is the "who" you are when you are just being you.

3. The Attitude number: This number is found by adding your month of birth to your day of birth and reducing it to a single digit. Your Attitude number's definition offers insight into your feelings and sensitivities, actions and reactions to your parents, and other environmental stimuli in your childhood, teen, and early adult years. The influence of this attitude usually begins to diminish between the ages of 30 to 35 as you evolve into adulthood. At that time, the Destiny, Personality, and Character numbers begin to have much greater power and influence over your "inside" and "outside" personas.

THE THREE NUMBERS DERIVED FROM YOUR NAME

4. The Character number: This number is found by adding together, and reducing to a single digit, the numbers associated with the letters in your name from birth. It represents your most public self, i.e.; the persona you exhibit at social gatherings, in the workplace, or at school. It also influences how you express your innate talents and capabilities, as well as the personality qualities you exhibit when you feel uncomfortable with your surroundings. It is the "who" you present when you are outside your most comfortable surroundings.

5. The Soul Urge number: This number is found by adding together, and reducing to a single digit, the numbers associated with the vowels in your name from birth. The Soul Urge represents the "burning desire" (or most soulful desire) behind your public persona. Its number definition offers insight as to "why" you express yourself as you do in public.

6. The Hidden Agenda number: This number is found by adding together, and reducing to a single digit, the numbers associated with the consonants in your name from birth. Its vibration is not as powerful as the Character and Soul Urge number vibrations. It, therefore, represents your secret desires and aspirations. The Hidden Agenda is the "what" you would hope to gain by exhibiting the best qualities of the Character and Soul Urge numbers. Sometimes discovering the influence of your Hidden Agenda can be more of a surprise to you than to anyone else.

As you go through this book, keep in mind that numbers are neither good nor bad. Each one has both positive and negative aspects. Each one works with the others to create a complete picture of who you are, and it can take a long time before a student of this science is able to pull all the numbers together and interpret them in a comprehensive way. This book was written in the hopes of making that process easier and faster.

Chapter 3
The Destiny Numbers
The Most Influential Number in Relation to Your Life's Path

Of all your numbers, this one has the most powerful influence on your life. It is the compelling force within you that causes you to gravitate toward a certain lifestyle or career. It spawns an attraction to certain types of people, including your lovers and friends, and specific social activities. What you like in your surroundings, from furniture to ambiance, and how you acclimate to your environs are also affected by this dominant energy force. It is the strongest *motivational* force in your life and, as such, it has been assigned to the center position in the Wizard's Star (see Chapter 5 for more about the Wizard's Star).

To determine your Destiny number, add all the numbers in your birth date together and reduce them to a single digit.

For example, if you were born on November 24, 1980, you would add, as follows: 1 + 1 (November) + 2 + 4 + 1 + 9 + 8 + 0 = 26 and then add 2 + 6 = 8. The Destiny number for this birth date is 8. (Note: To determine if your birth date reduces to a Master number [11 or 22], it is suggested that you use both methods of addition referred to in Chapter 2. If a Master number can be obtained from either method, read the definitions for both the 2 and the 11, or the 4 and the 22, to determine which one best fits you or the person you know.)

My Destiny Number Is: _____

DESTINY NUMBER 1

The path of the risk-taker, the entrepreneur, the wholly independent trailblazer.

THE GOOD NEWS

You came into this life to be as autonomous as possible, and this Destiny number ensures that you have what it takes to call your own shots and run your own show. Most of you recognized this at a very early age since, even as children, it was probably difficult for you to take orders from anyone. One-Destiny people are powerful, independent, charming, and loaded with innate talent!

You are the most original, pioneering, and innovative of all the destiny numbers, and when you are interested enough to be one of the best in your career endeavor or hobby, you *are*! Like Tiger Woods, Kristie Yamaguchi, Tom Hanks, Ronnie Lott, and Ernest Hemingway, you can rise to the top of your field—receiving honors and admiration from your peers—*if you are properly challenged!*

You also have a mind like a steel trap regarding subject matter that interests you. This asset helps you to be a very formidable debater should the opportunity arise. Your vast knowledge also makes you hard to beat at games like Trivial Pursuit or working crossword puzzles.

You are the most competitive people on the planet and, because of your winner-takes-all attitude, you do not like to lose at anything (including love). In fact, most of you won't even participate in a game—be it a board game or something more competitive, like tennis or golf—unless you think you can outmaneuver or outplay the other players. It's reasonable to say that when you are personally motivated to win, you can be like a steamroller—virtually flattening anything or anyone who might try to impede your ultimate goal. You truly can be an undauntable and indestructible force—when you *want* to be!

AT HOME

You have traditional values, and you like to be viewed as someone who plays the social game well. However, most of you will effect your own original approach to what the rest of society might consider acceptable behavior.

You are just too independent to follow the dictates of a "majority rule." You are conservative and traditional about certain aspects of your family life, like how children should be raised and the kind of values you teach them. Yet you can be quite liberal and sometimes even radical in your political views and about anything that affects your personal freedom.

To say that 1-Destiny people are private about their personal life is an understatement. Your privacy issues are directly linked to your desire to be in control of every facet of your own life. You tend to be cautious around and suspicious of others, especially when you first meet them. You often find it difficult to trust people, even with information that may seem insignificant to some, like how old you are. Many of you play at life as you would a chess game, calculating every move to outmaneuver your opposition so that all "plays" or possibilities are covered.

Most of you have a multitude of varied interests. You might be a wine connoisseur or a superb gourmet cook, an animal breeder (1-Destiny people especially like the obedient nature of dogs), or a history buff. If you have a hobby, it is usually something that is all-consuming because when you thoroughly enjoy something, you know no half-measures. You tend to be "all or nothing" in your approach to everything.

Neither male nor female 1s have much interest in domesticity. Washing the dishes and scrubbing the bathroom are better left to those who haven't come into this life to be action-takers, leaders, or Doers with a capital D. When it comes to domesticity, you are far more skilled at relegating and delegating than taking a "hands-on" approach to such tasks. And, if you can't avoid being your own housekeeper, you will most assuredly find your own unique way to cook and clean!

AT WORK

As previously stated, the vast majority of 1-Destiny people virtually come into this life desiring the greatest amount of independence and autonomy there is. It is therefore imperative, if you are to be a "happy camper" in the workplace, that you either own your own business or are in a position of autonomy and independence when working for someone else. You are not team players, and if you work for someone who doesn't exhibit your level of agility, dexterity, or mental prowess, you will have difficulty respecting and/or taking orders from him/her. It is essential, when you are working for someone else, that you are given some personal latitude on the job. One problem may be, however, that in cases where you don't like your work, you are likely to take great advantage of that latitude.

Teaching is one profession that can offer you the stability you crave, along with the ability to use your originality and feel relatively independent at the same time. The computer field is another area in which the innovative 1-Destiny individual can express his/her originality and have a semblance of autonomy as an employee. Steven Jobs, the founder and current CEO of Apple Computers, is a good example of someone who has used the personal qualities of the 1-Destiny to his advantage.

If you are a typical 1-Destiny person, you will have to discover the golden well of talent within you by yourself because *no one* can influence you in any way regarding your likes and dislikes or in choosing your profession. You are the bottom-line decision-maker in your life, and you either *really* like something (or someone) or you just can't be bothered—and that attitude permeates all areas of your life.

SOCIALLY

One-Destiny women tend to be more social than their male counterparts. However, some of the women also lack the inclination to seek out social or community get-togethers and events. When either sex shows up on the social scene, you can be among the most charming and interesting people in attendance. You know how to play the social game; it's just the obligatory social chitchat that drives you nuts—and the possibility of getting stuck talking with people who bore you. If you feel a personal responsibility to join a certain social group for career or community purposes, then you will usually wend your way into a leadership position as a way of avoiding the mundane "worker-bee" sort of tasks.

Most 1-Destiny people are well-known in their social environment as individuals who have strong opinions and independent ways. Those who know you well would never presume to assign you to a committee or make other decisions about you without first ensuring that you were amenable.

At the same time, once you do commit to something, you get things done with great speed and efficiency.

If there is a time when a 1-Destiny person will be uncharacteristically social, it is during the holidays. Since 1s are great traditionalists, the holidays hold a significant place in your hearts. You can be especially sentimental about your childhood experiences with regard to holidays, and you enjoy reviving the best aspects of those memories with decorations, food, ceremonies, and rituals.

FRIENDSHIP AND LOVE

One-Destiny people are very loyal to their friends. In fact, they may keep in touch with a childhood friend for life. You find the greatest affinity with those who are as strong-willed and independent as you are. Most of you have little inclination to join the coffee klatch group or the social go-getters, and you definitely steer clear of anyone who needs your constant approval and/or attention.

When you fall in love, you fall hard because you tend to take your time analyzing (and sometimes researching) potential love partners. Both sexes are most attracted to strong, independent types who challenge your control issues. Seeking someone who is as independent as you are is good in some ways, but problems can ensue when one or the other of you wants their partner to change or attempts to set rules for them to follow. Even though most of you feel a sense of excitement by challenge, you are better off seeking a mate who is accommodating to your needs. After the "hunt and capture" phase has passed, a relationship with a less challenging mate will bring you both more contentment. Some couples, when both parties are strong and independent, have long-lasting standoffs when disagreements arise. Refer to the compatibility chart in Chapter 6 for those Destiny numbers that are best suited to your nature.

THE NOT-SO-GOOD NEWS
UNFOUNDED FEARS

Some of you are so fearful of losing control of your future that you deny your inherent risk-taker nature and go through life wishing you had the courage to break out of your self-imposed boundaries in the workplace or in a relationship/marriage you dislike. The archives of the famous and influential are filled with people with 1-Destinies who have risked everything for one major goal and beat the odds. You have what it takes to join their ranks! YOU DO—if you will simply focus on doing something you thoroughly enjoy—every day!

CONFLICT AT WORK

Because you are so independent and unique, some of you can sabotage your ability to connect with the things that inspire you the most because you won't focus long enough to develop the superlative talents you possess. Many of you pass up the opportunity to complete a college degree because you like the freedom of being out of school. All of you are late bloomers and, as such, it can take you much longer than some others to find your nich. In fact, many of you will make radical changes in your careers after the age of 35.

STRUGGLES WITH INDEPENDENCE

A great many of you have difficulty taking orders from others. This can result in your moving from job to job or settling for a job you don't really like just because it gives you a degree of independence or autonomy. This inability to find a job that really suits you is common among people with 1-Destinies. All of you are destined to learn to stand on your own in a strong and courageous way at some point in your lives. If you haven't entered a field that gives you personal gratification by the age of 35, most of you will find a way to work for yourselves—or at least work more independently after that age. Age 36 is when you enter the second phase of your life, and that is when you begin to feel more emphatically the need to be as independent as possible.

SOCIAL NEGATIVES

Most of you are very private about your personal and business lives and resent anyone meddling in your affairs. As a consequence, you are sometimes considered aloof, standoffish, and even antisocial. You all have the potential to be leaders, but when you fail to meet the high goals you set for yourselves (usually because you didn't give enough focus or effort), you look for an easier, faster way to meet your needs. In fact, you can be as formidable in the underworld as you may be respected by conventional society. Hopefully, by reading this book and learning how exceptional you can be when you find the right focus, you will be better able to let your higher side reign.

SELFISH AND CONTROLLING NATURE

Some of you get so caught up in yourselves and your own needs that you become controlling, selfish, closed off, and shut down, and you create dissension and animosity wherever you go. At your worst, you can become dictatorial and domineering taskmasters, and you can even develop into extraordinary liars and cheats!

MOTIVATIONAL PROJECT

By now you should realize that to be fulfilled in your career you must connect with what you *love the most*, that which gives you the *greatest autonomy* and uses your abilities to be *original, innovative, and a leader*. Once you have found your niche and have pursued it with steadfast commitment, money and success should follow.

We all express some positive and some negative aspects of our numbers at different times, so don't be too hard on yourself if you identify with a few of the negative traits mentioned above. However, if you identify with *more* negative traits than positive ones, it's probably time for you to start rearranging your priorities. You know better than anyone that when you set a goal for yourself, you always find a way to achieve it, even if it's not in your best interest. You will plow through everything and anything that gets in your way until you have accomplished what you set out to do. You can, in fact, become quite ruthless and relentless when you make a decision to get to the top or to have your way. This can diminish much of the positive power inherent in this dynamic Destiny vibration.

To start today to discover your real "passions," it is suggested that you clear your mind and begin to think about what you would do if you could be anything you want. Would you become an artist, a dancer, a building contractor, an architect, a newsreporter, a fiction-writer, a professional athlete? With the 1 as your Destiny number, you *could* do any one of those things very, very well!

DESTINY NUMBER 2

The path of the homemaker, the team player, the caretaker, and the collector.

NOTE: It is important to use both methods of addition given in Chapter 2 to calculate this Destiny number. You may discover that your Destiny number reduces to a 2 with one method and to an 11 with the other. In that case, it is suggested that you read both the 2-Destiny number definitions as well as the definitions associated with the 11-Destiny. (Most people whose Destiny number reduces to the Master number 11 have as much affinity with qualities of the 2-Destiny as they do the 11-Destiny).

THE GOOD NEWS

You respond to your surroundings and the people in it with warmth, affection, compassion, and a depth of understanding. You are a good listener and have an earnest desire to help anyone in need. You will easily set aside your own desires or needs in favor of someone else's, and you enjoy giving more than receiving.

The number 2 is the most nurturing of all the numbers, and its vibration summons forth the impulses of a coddling mother or protective father. Most everyone with a 2-Destiny is gentle, considerate, diplomatic, sympathetic, and a natural caretaker. You are also cooperative, a peacemaker, and a team player. Your non-aggressive, congenial style makes it easy for others to enjoy your company and, as a consequence, your life is filled with many friends and social invitations.

You are kind to everyone, and those who are fortunate enough to be invited into your home experience your sincere generosity and gracious hospitality. Because of your honest desire to please others, you attract few, if any, enemies in your lifetime.

AT HOME

You desire serene, harmonious surroundings, and your peace-loving posture helps to inspire that kind of essence. Your home is usually decorated in a style that effects comfort and ease. As music lovers, you fill the 2-Destiny home with music-playing devices, and cassette tapes, CDs, and DVDs of your favorite sounds. Some of you play a musical instrument, or sing and dance as a hobby, and all of you are great fans of entertainment that features those performing arts. In fact, music is essential to your well-being and helps to give you a sense of balance and keep you grounded. The more music you have in your life, the merrier you are!

Most 2-Destiny people enjoy collecting and displaying personal mementos, souvenirs, antiques, and other memorabilia. Your surroundings may be a menagerie of odds and ends, or a sensuous, luxurious environment with expensive artifacts and pricey collectibles. Because of your romantic nature, most of you like to decorate your bedrooms in an especially sensuous and lush manner.

Many of you are superlative cooks, and your greatest pleasure is watching your family and friends consume your sumptuous concoctions. Whoever proffered the adage, "Eat, drink and be merry," must surely have been someone with a 2-Destiny.

Being a caretaker is a natural proclivity of all 2-Destiny people. So, whether it's your spouse or your own children, an extended family or friends, volunteering with your church or helping with some other community program, most of you eventually wend your way into some kind of service work—much to the benefit of others.

AT WORK

You are team players and natural arbiters, and you have the ability to clearly understand both sides of any disagreement or problem. Many U.S. presidents and foreign leaders have this Destiny number, as do other dignitaries, lawyers, counselors, and therapists.

Another positive quality of this Destiny number is that most of you can work behind the scenes, even doing menial and mundane tasks for those of higher rank, without feeling sad that you are not in the spotlight. Your cooperative, easily adaptable nature makes it simple for anyone to work with or for you.

Because 2-Destiny people like to nurture and be of service, many of you gravitate to careers in the hospitality field, such as working in hotels, for the airlines, or other highly public domains. The ocean (which is ruled by the number 2 vibration) also has a strong appeal to you, and many of you find careers on ships or with cruise lines. Other fulfilling career options for this Destiny include caring for children and seniors, such as working in day-care centers or performing home services; owning and operating restaurants or catering businesses, or working in some other capacity in the food industry; business administration and management; sales, especially of items that are useful in the home or bring comfort and aid to people; writing romance novels (all 2-Destiny people are romantics), or acting (even though this Destiny doesn't vie for the stage, most of you are natural hams and enjoy entertaining others).

SOCIALLY

Although you can be homebodies, you are also very people-oriented. Entertaining at home may be one of your favorite activities, but you cannot go long before you are out and about, mingling with the masses. Most of you belong to clubs and participate in numerous social activities and events. You are comfortable in almost any setting, from attending the ballet to getting together with your best buds for a sporting event.

Another distinguishing social trait of this Destiny number is your penchant for pampering yourself. Luxuriating at health spas, dining in fine restaurants, and traveling to exotic places are some of the things that give you your greatest personal pleasures.

FRIENDSHIP AND LOVE

You are the type who thinks of others first. Most of you remember your friends and relatives on special occasions with greeting cards or other mementos of affection and friendship. Giving comes naturally to you but, as mentioned above, you are also an appreciative receiver and especially fond of keepsake items.

Your friends tend to be kind, caring souls like you. Your best love match is someone who is nurturing and giving, too, because otherwise your romance can become unbalanced as you do all the giving while your partner takes, takes, takes. Small wonder that one-sided relationships like that often tilt and topple over.

Many of you attract people with problems into your life because you are such good listeners and you can easily set yourself up to be the "big shoulders" and sympathetic ears for anyone who needs some understanding. Your natural gift for counseling and ministering to people makes it difficult for you to turn away anyone who needs a helping hand or someone to listen to their problems—and you can be some of the most responsible, nurturing, and accommodating parents and mates.

THE NOT-SO-GOOD NEWS
PERSONALITY AND HOME LIFE

When you express the negative qualities of this Destiny number, you can be meddlesome, over-sensitive, fault-finding, discourteous, and inconsiderate. Yes, you can exhibit qualities that are just the opposite of the "angel-like" attributes referred to under The Good News. That's because every number has its high side and its low side. The following paragraphs present other, less attractive traits of this Destiny number, along with ways to diminish their power, should you desire to do so.

VACILLATION AND CONFORMATION

Your ability to see both sides of every situation, disagreement, or problem can have a mind-numbing effect on some of you. It can cause you to vacillate about everything until the cows come home! Your desire for peace and harmony, and your need to please others, can also backfire by causing you to conform to everyone and everything in your atmosphere to such a degree that you lose any idea of who you really are and what you actually like or don't like. If you have this wishy-washy nature, it is suggested that when a new situation arises and you feel compelled to weigh the pros and cons, you try to determine what YOU really feel or think. Your friends may like the fact that you always agree with whatever they say and that you try to accommodate their every desire, but it's better for YOU to have your own opinion, on occasion, by offering a definitive "yes" or "no."

OVERLY EMOTIONAL

Another negative effect of this Destiny number is that some of you can be super-sensitive, highly emotional, and moody. If you identify with this temperament, it is likely that you are not nurturing yourself enough or getting your own needs met. Regardless of what problems you face, when there is an imbalance in your life between your needs and your wants, your body and your psyche will react in some way. You may find yourself suffering from frequent headaches or from some other kind of physical ailment, or you may be depressed or angry. Two-Destiny people need a lot of gentle, loving care. You are the "touchy, feely" people of the Destiny chain. Being hugged, and especially hugging back, helps you to feel more alive and healthier. Other things that help 2-Destiny people feel better when you are in a funk are massages, baths, long nature walks, and listening to your favorite music (which brings your sensitive equilibrium into balance). The most important advice for you is to do something every day that makes you feel good about being YOU.

BEING NEEDY AND/OR WITHHOLDING AFFECTION

Many 2-Destiny people who haven't used the power within to get what they need from life, become overly needy of others. You can become an attention monger, needing constant reassurance from friends and family that they are there for you. Or, even worse, you can become a martyr or sniveler, complaining that no one ever does for you what you do for others. It is a fact that no one else is capable of making you feel better. Only you can do that. Unless you have clinical depression (and need medication), feeling better about your life can definitely come from developing a positive attitude. Take an objective look at the role you might be playing in creating some of the disparities that exist in your life. Sometimes, when you get overly needy, you can fail to see that it is your *own* attitude that needs to change.

Many of you keep your sentimental and sensitive nature to yourself, and some of you will withhold the very things that mean the most to you—like affection and caretaking. This can be an attempt to "get even" with those you feel haven't given you the appreciation you think you deserve. Once again, when you start feeling that someone owes you something, you block your ability to be honest with yourself, and you can't see the role you play in helping to create your negative feelings.

CONFLICT AT WORK

If you do not get the appreciation you feel you deserve at work, you can become moody and unresponsive to your co-workers and boss. Most 2-Destiny people desire appreciation more than anything. You do not normally crave the spotlight or care about whether others defer to you. But you do want to be appreciated for what you DO do. Receiving a "thank you" is something everyone appreciates, but if you are not acknowledged in that way occasionally, over time you can become quite irascible.

If you feel unappreciated at work, decide that it is up to you to appreciate yourself. The people who find it difficult to show you their appreciation are usually too busy focusing on themselves anyway. Challenge yourself to be the best you can be, and in the process, you will be giving yourself tremendous gratification and appreciation—a gift *from* you *to* you!

Appreciation is one of the reasons that 2-Destiny people gravitate to service careers. Even though people in service capacities may not be thanked every minute of the day, they are likely to receive that kind of acknowledgment more frequently than [when you are employed] in other occupations.

MOTIVATIONAL PROJECT

If your life feels unfulfilled in any way, it is probably time to bump yourself out of your comfort zone and do something to improve or expand yourself. Think about which area of your life needs the most urgent attention -— your education, your career, your home life, your personal life, your spiritual life, or your health. Choose the one that is currently giving you the least satisfaction and then set a definitive goal to make it better. Set just one goal in the beginning that isn't too time-consuming or arduous.

That way, you're likely to give yourself a psychological boost by seeing some immediate improvement. Also, if you do one thing at a time, or as much as you feel you can handle comfortably, and stick to it until it is accomplished, before long you will begin to feel a renewed sense of power and strength that will push you toward achieving all your other goals!

DESTINY NUMBER 3

The path of the adventurous, proverbial "Peter Pan," or the disciplined "Dapper Dan/Danielle."

THE GOOD NEWS

Those of you with a 3-Destiny are fated to have good fortune throughout your lives. That's right—no matter how you might be manifesting this Destiny number, there will always be a helping hand or a windfall that will come your way—even in the eleventh hour, when all may seem lost. Having good fortune is your birthright! Lucky you!

Three-Destiny people are born enthusiasts. You are optimistic and usually quite enchanted by life—and that nature tends to endure into your senior years. The majority of you are drawn to the arts, the theater, and anything that has to do with entertainment. You have a somewhat child-like approach to life—always conjuring up ways to make your life more exciting and adventuresome or, at the very least, enjoyable and pleasurable.

AT HOME

Many of you are fastidious with regard to your surroundings, your attire, and what you eat and drink. "Everything in its place, and a place for everything," is a credo by which many of you live. If you identify with this nature, you gravitate to the "disciplined" side of this Destiny number. On the other hand, some 3s are quite laid-back with regard to neatness and orderliness. If you identify with this, you are the "artistic" 3-Destiny type. Even though the artistic 3 may have messy or disorganized surroundings, he/she also uses the precision-oriented tendencies of their disciplined side to produce incredible pieces of artwork, prose, or other ingenious compositions. The disciplined 3-Destiny type can also show their artistic and creative talents in their home decor or effect something wonderfully creative in their careers. To some degree, most of you do, in fact, actualize both the artistic and the disciplined aspects of this Destiny number.

Whether you are a neat-nick or a veritable slob in your home or at the office, most of you like to expend the least amount of effort for the most amount of gain and, therefore, will have appliances and gadgets in your home and office that make life easier and more efficient. You do not get a charge out of housecleaning or puttering about doing home chores. Instead, you prefer to be active outside the home, mingling with others or traveling hither and yon, staging gala events or doing anything that is exciting and different.

As parents, you are disciplinarians, but you can also enjoy most of the activities your children seem to like. Parents who love to take the scariest rides with their children at amusement parks likely have 3-Destinies. Most of you love adventure of any type. You are also wonderful storytellers and can hold the attention of a flock of children by using your extraordinary imagination to enhance childhood fairy tales or, even better, your own wild and woolly tales.

AT WORK

You like to work as independently as possible and, most importantly, you need to garner some kind of excitement or pleasure out of your work or you will, as stated above, expend the least amount of effort for the most amount of gain. You do not enjoy laborious or physically demanding jobs. You are happiest working in a career that enables you to network and bring together interesting people and ideas. Most of you believe you can accomplish the impossible, and many of you *do*! As a consequence, you are especially well-suited to occupations that give you the latitude to use your energized and self-assured nature to spur others on to greater heights. You can be exceptional elementary school teachers because of your inspirational proclivities.

Some 3-Destiny people may not identify with the joie de vivre characteristics of the 3. You may not be as exuberant and enthusiastic about life as are most of your fellow 3-Destiny folks. Some of you get so engrossed in your goals and careers that you fail to have ANY fun. If you identify with being a more serious individual in relation to your work and your personal habits, you are probably someone who has found a profession that provides you with a certain degree of control while, at the same time, a sense of adventure, inspiration, and intrigue. Many athletes, accountants, computer whizzes, scientists, and physicists fall under this category. Each of those professions requires an exacting and dedicated attitude, and many with a 3-Destiny exude those qualities.

SOCIALLY

Most of you are the consummate hosts and hostesses. You love to entertain and be entertained, and you have a penchant for bringing together the most unique and interesting props and people. When you are manifesting this side of your Destiny number, everyone benefits because you set out to make sure that they do! You are "assembly line artists," being almost obsessive about getting everything in order before the guests arrive. As a consequence, many of you are called upon or volunteer to help friends or social organizations to orchestrate parties and events. In fact, being an event coordinator is an excellent occupation for those of you who derive pleasure out of this natural talent.

Along with being superb social partisans, as mentioned above, you are also skilled networkers. You thoroughly enjoy having something to promote or champion. Even if your Character or Personality numbers are less inclined to display take-charge characteristics, the motto of most 3-Destiny people is "the more, the merrier." That sentiment inspires you to spread the word to one and all about your latest, interesting connection or upcoming event.

Some of you are also great adventure aficionados—always looking for something more electrifying or thrilling than your last experience. You are well-known for your willingness to try ANYTHING at least once and, if it made you feel good, you will come back for more! Because of this nature, you may find it difficult to ever be completely content to act like a grownup, and many of you have more fun with kids than with adults. And, children like you, too—especially when you entertain them with your colorful and enthusiastic imagination.

FRIENDSHIP AND LOVE

When you are in love, your wonderful imagination can dream up the most exciting and romantic plans and rendezvous. It is unlikely that anyone would ever be disappointed [in] a romantic getaway created by Mr. or Ms. 3-Destiny. Some people make things special, but you make almost every experience exceptional and extraordinary! You are never at a loss for interesting places to go, things to do, or people to see, but you can also be very content spending a quiet evening or weekend in the exclusive company of your special someone. There IS a serene, cuddly side of you that is as delightful as your more adventuresome side. However, anyone wishing to be your lifetime companion better be as adventurous and independent as you are because you will not be content to sit quietly in the confines of your home for long. If your mate doesn't have what it takes to keep up with you, you are perfectly content to do your own thing all by yourself! Right? Right!

As a friend, you can be the most encouraging, inspiring, and fun-loving person there is. You are always ready to drop what you're doing and run, drive, or fly to the aid of a friend or family member. Your undauntable spirit and robust enthusiasm for life attract chums who either have the same qualities you do or who want to be around someone who does. You gather people into your life easily, and you usually retain your friends forever.

THE BEST NEWS

The Good News is that the majority of those with a 3-Destiny find ways to do and be whatever makes them feel good or fulfilled. And, THE BEST NEWS IS that all of you possess the talents and capabilities to accomplish your goals—especially if you gravitate to the high side of this auspicious Destiny number, as explained above.

Finally, it is the author's belief that everyone should have at least one 3-Destiny person in their life to inspire them, by example, to have a more positive and personally courageous attitude.

THE NOT-SO-GOOD NEWS
THE DRILL SERGEANT

There is another side to the grand host/hostess disposition, which is being overly picky and exacting. A meticulous nature certainly helps you pull off grand affairs and parties, but it can also turn you into a precision-oriented drill sergeant. You may become overly critical of those who have difficulty marching to your drumbeat or of those who don't live by your stringent rules of hygiene, nutrition, and impeccable grooming. This drill sergeant quality can permeate every facet of your life, from home to the office, and even in your social life. You may not only be picky about your *own* personal appearance but also that of everyone else in your surroundings, (some of you will notice a fleck of dandruff on someone's lapel the moment they come into your view); and you sometimes find it difficult to keep from "fixing" what you view as other people's flaws with their appearance or personality.

OVER-DISCIPLINARY AS PARENTS

It is usually a priority of 3-Destiny parents to train their children to be well-mannered, efficient, and disciplined and, even though you enjoy acting like a kid yourself occasionally, you can be a strong taskmaster on the home front. And woe to your mate if he or she doesn't adhere to your standard of orderliness and efficiency! When this demanding nature gets carried to an extreme, you can become a nag and an authoritarian which, needless to say, can be very destructive for your relationships at home and in the workplace. If you identify with this nature, try to recognize that you are not perfect either. That may be difficult for some of you to do because when your authoritarian nature rules, you may begin to think that you know what is best for everyone and that you simply can't be wrong about *anything*! Can you imagine how frustrating it would be to live with someone like that?

CHILDISH NATURE

As mentioned earlier, some with 3-Destinies can be downright childish—never picking up after yourselves, avoiding responsibility of any kind, and always looking for or needing someone to take care of you and your needs. Being lazy is another strong indicator of someone with a 3-Destiny who gravitates to the lowest side of this vibration. When this childish nature prevails, you may also have a tendency to be over-indulgent with food and drink and, in some instances, you may even be considered a "party-girl" or "party-boy."

GIVING WITH STRINGS ATTACHED

Although most of you are known to be extremely generous, whether picking up the check for dinner, gift giving to friends and family, or praising someone else's accomplishments or talent, a small faction of you use your giving nature to gain more attention for yourself. Those of you who have this tendency desire to be the *shining star* in everyone's life, and you do and say things that will turn the spotlight on you. Some of you even vie for adoration and idolatry from others, and, in the process, you may try to establish your own entourage of personal admirers.

Another aspect of this nature involves giving because of what you'll get out of it. This goes hand-in-hand with a personality that needs constant accolades and praise from others. Those of you who identify with this description may think it's perfectly fine to be that way. You may feel that *everyone*, after all, benefits by your generosity. If you have this attitude, you may need to look at the possibility that your generosity is motivated by excessive vanity and/or an exaggerated ego.

MOTIVATIONAL PROJECT

In order for anyone with a 3-Destiny to be completely happy in life, you must have an occupation that gives you a feeling of exhilaration and independence. Because many of you like the precision and orderliness of math and science, you make good accountants, physicists, and computer technicians. More likely, however, you will gravitate to a career that involves working with or serving the public in some way because of your strong people-oriented nature. A career in one of the arts is another viable possibility because the majority of you are either artistic or drawn to every facet of the arts in your personal lives. As a matter of fact, a great many accomplished actors, writers, and fine painters have 3-Destinies.

Most 3-Destiny people are the classic late-bloomers, so if you haven't connected with a career that gives you a feeling of unrelenting *joy*, don't be discouraged. Being complacent is not an option for most 3-Destiny types, unless you've found that pot of gold at the end of the rainbow that all 3s dream about. It is essential that you set a goal for yourself to find the career that gives you the utmost personal satisfaction. Once you identify what that might be, you should pursue it with all your energy. You can give so much to the world by doing the thing that makes you happiest because when you are content, you are an inspiration to others and usually create something that *everyone* can enjoy.

DESTINY NUMBER 4

The path of the hard-working, kind-hearted, honest, and dedicated "Rock of Gibralter."

NOTE: To determine whether you have a 4-Destiny or a 22-Destiny, it is suggested that you use both methods of addition for the birth date in Chapter 2 (the horizontal method and the vertical method). You may find that you derive a 4-Destiny with one method and a 22 with the other. In that case, it is suggested that you read the definitions for both the 4 and the 22. (Those whose Destiny number reduces to a 22 have as much of an affinity with the qualities of 4-Destiny as does a 4-Destiny person to the qualities of the 22-Destiny.)

THE GOOD NEWS

This Destiny number contains such a super-charged vibration that it could turn you into a Success with a capital S! Like your 4-Destiny counterparts Bill Gates, Oprah Winfrey, and Donald Trump, when you have a passion for something, you have the potential to build an empire! However, it may not be that easy for you to rise to the ranks of Bill, Oprah or Donald, because they primarily resonate to the highest vibration of the 4—the Master number 22. Nonetheless, all of you possess a strong work ethic, organizational abilities, and the innate determination to take yourself over-the-top in any field you choose. Regardless of whether you achieve high honors, experience monumental monetary gains, or live a simple, quiet, hard-working existence, most of you feel compelled to do something to serve or help mankind and the earth. As a matter of fact, one of the missions of someone with a 4-Destiny is to help others. It is a natural impulse that goes with your life's path, and you can't (and shouldn't) avoid it.

AT HOME

Regardless of whether you are a homemaker, a forest ranger, or a rock star, you *give one hundred percent!* When you accept a responsibility, a job, or a duty, most of you are ready, willing, and able to fulfill its requirements. Your industriousness and conscientious work efforts contribute a great deal to the overall physical comfort and stability of your family, your home, and sometimes even the community at large. Because most of you give so much in the workplace, you don't relish the responsibilities of the domestic part of your life. You are especially averse to things like slaving over a hot stove after work to make family meals, or doing chores and duties around the house on weekends! But, because of your orderly nature, you won't tolerate disarray in your surroundings for very long.

Honesty and fairness in all things is important to 4-Destiny people, and you are not inclined to become martyrs. Although you don't tend to harbor feelings of martyrdom or blame others for your problems, when you do have something to say, you are not known for having much tact or diplomacy. In fact, if someone has offended you, or if you feel compelled to defend something in which you firmly believe, you can express yourself in a very forthright manner—preferring to say what you think the instant you *think* it! You may even derive pleasure from forcing others to address issues that they would prefer to ignore. Once you have expounded on your feelings, you are usually through with the matter (until the next time it comes up, that is).

Many of you become completely involved in your hobbies since once you find something you enjoy, you can't get enough of it! If you are not as happy as you would like to be at home or on-the-job, you may direct your focus and energies into something on the outside, like golf, rock climbing, or a creative endeavor.

AT WORK

Most of you are the like the "Rock of Gibraltar" in most areas of your life, but this is especially true of the workplace. Your word is gold, and your strong work ethic, honesty, and punctuality are qualities that make you a superlative employee. In fact, some of you would rather work than do anything else, and this attitude makes you a good candidate to be self-employed. All of your positive attributes make you entrepreneurial material, and no one (other than yourself) will *ever* pay you what you deserve for the time and effort you expend on your job. So, if you don't have your own business yet, and you do not like your current job, you might begin to think about how you could get into your own business one day. You will not work any less; in fact, you will probably work more, and you may not even get paid as much as you receive from an employer. But you will probably find the freedom of being your own boss and feeling appreciated by your clients more fulfilling. Remember though, if you like your job and your employer, there's a strong likelihood that your employer really appreciates and likes you, too!

SOCIALLY

Most of you tend to be down-to-earth, and you dislike pretensions or pomp and circumstance. And, although you can enjoy the cultured life, you are more comfortable in your own confines, enjoying the company of good friends and family, than you are being out on the town. Fundamentally, you like gatherings of people who share your wholesome approach to life and hold similar ideals.

Many of you find a way to work while you socialize. Whether you are a bartender or an entertainer, your vocation may provide you with your favorite way to socialize because you *do* so love to work!

FRIENDSHIP AND LOVE

As a friend, you are loyal and always ready to help others in whatever way you can. Dependable and reliable, you *always* honor your commitments. Although the majority of 4-Destiny people like to entertain and be entertained at home, as mentioned earlier, some of you are also avid hobbyists, and you meet and make many of your friends through your hobbies. Your loyal and consistent demeanor makes you a prize as a friend!

In love, you tend to do more than your share of giving. People with needs gravitate to you because of your giving nature, and some of you have to learn the hard way how to say no to those you love. Your self-sufficiency and ability to earn a good wage make it easy for you to overspend on yourself and others. Most of you have simple wants and needs, but your romantic life (or home life, if you don't have a love-mate) is where you reward yourself big time! If you have a craving for something, you will get it, and anyone who is lucky enough to share your "rewards" is in for a bountiful ride!

You may not be publicly affectionate, but you are definitely interested in the physical side of love. Most of you have a robust and indefatigable lovemaking nature and, when you want to be, you can be very warm and hard to resist.

THE NOT-SO-GOOD NEWS
LAZYBONES

Many of you can be utterly lazy when you don't have anything pressing at the office or on your work agenda. When you are in the comfortable confines of your home, you may not be inclined to do much at all. In fact, you can be downright boring for those who live with you because you're not someone who enjoys the nightlife either.

OBSESSION WITH DETAILS

Many of you are very exacting and can become obsessed with details, sometimes failing to see the proverbial "forest for the trees." In fact, you may get so caught up in the small picture that you sabotage your efforts to create a substantial business or career, thinking that you don't have enough money, or enough talent, or enough of anything else that's needed. What you *do* have is enough honesty, determination, conscientiousness, responsibility, and dedication. Those are all qualities that make you a better employee, employer, or business owner than almost anyone else!

BEING STUBBORN

As mentioned above, 4-Destiny people tend to be stubborn and sometimes immovable. Most of you are also "No" kinds of people. "No, I don't want to," or "No, I can't do that," or "No, that's not what I like," or simply, "No, forget

it." In other words, you are not inclined to be very spontaneous, if spontaneous at all! You want to be given time to think things over before moving
in any direction. Even as children, your parents usually learned early that
you needed to believe you were making your own decisions or you simply
would not do anything they wanted you to do—even if you secretly wanted
to do it. If you have a 2/11, 3, 5, or 6 as one of your other primary numbers
(the Character, Personality, or Attitude), then you may be more inclined
to release yourself from your self-imposed cellblock of stubbornness. But if
you have another 4 in one of these positions, you may be virtually impossible to deal with, especially when you are young.

THE GRAND DEBATER

The 4 is the number of the contrarian, and contrary you can be! Many
of you like to take the opposite side of virtually *any* topic of conversation
(even if you *agree* with the general premise being presented), just for the
sake of debate. You are extraordinary fact-collectors, and some of you enjoy
brandishing about insignificant facts or erudite knowledge whenever possible. You are not pretentious, but you can present yourself in a very
iconoclastic fashion that causes major discomfort or frustration for anyone
who disagrees with your position.

THE SAVIOR

Many 4-Destiny people try to be saviors to those who appear unable to
help themselves. You actually seek out people who have been victimized or
are down on their luck—and, as everyone knows, they are not hard to find.
This seemingly noble leaning can sometimes be quite detrimental to the 4-
Destiny person's livelihood and lifestyle. Many times, this penchant is a
product of your own identification with the indigent and disenfranchised,
especially if you do your own personal "wild thing" for any period of time.
This savior tendency is inherent in this "giver" Destiny number. It is best,
however, if you choose to do volunteer work for a cause or organization
that is equipped to help people who are trying to save themselves. Trying
to save people before they are ready will invariably put you on the losing
end of the relationship—but then you probably know that already.

MOTIVATIONAL PROJECT

Most of you are hard-working, conscientious, responsible, dedicated, honest, and forthright. However, if you haven't yet actualized the driven and industrious side of your personality, it may be time for you to start getting serious about your career and future. Four-Destiny people usually enjoy reading non-fiction and self-help books. Go to your local bookstore or library and get some "positive mental attitude" books so you can begin the self-motivation process. It's time to stop trying to meet everyone else's needs without making sure you do the same for yourself! Anthony Robbins' book, *Awaken The Giant Within*, is an excellent source to help you get started with a positive plan for your life. Remember, you came here to give and, like Bill Gates and Oprah Winfrey, with the right plan or goal, you *could* be successful beyond your dreams!

DESTINY NUMBER 5

The path of the freedom fighter and the stylish and swinging social setter/world traveler.

THE GOOD NEWS

You are the movers and shakers of the universe. Highly adaptable and desiring constant change, diversity, and activity, you are always on the go—usually in the fast lane—heading from place to place in record time. You like to wear the latest styles (usually before the masses are even aware of them), tackle your business and personal obligations with unparalleled vim, vigor, and efficiency, and still have the energy reserves to participate in an active social and/or athletic life.

AT HOME

Some of you are not neat and tidy, but you are rare among your 5-Destiny fellows. Organization and proficiency are the most essential elements of your fast-paced lifestyle. Most of you can't allow yourselves the luxury of leaving the dishes unwashed or letting the laundry pile up because, for you, time is of the essence, and your life is packed full. Even though you will always drop what you are doing and rush to the aid of someone or something in need, you tend to have a multitude of things you volunteer to do, including exercise activities and family responsibilities— to say nothing of the myriad of at-home projects awaiting your dexterous and creative attention.

Women with 5-Destinies, more than 5 men, love to shop, but you do it with your usual fast pace. You know just where to go (and the fastest route to take) to get just what you need—usually in record time! Men exhibit the same M.O. when required to do the shopping, but they are less likely to look for the latest trends and fashions en route.

Five-Destiny people are spontaneous and sometimes impulsive, mainly because they like every minute to be as interesting as possible. They are also experts at finding ways to make every situation work out well for everyone involved. It is an understatement to say that most of you are highly energized, inspiring, and invigorating people.

AT WORK

As employees and employers, you are some of the best. Your greatest frustration is when you have to work with or for people who can't keep up with you—both mentally and physically. Your adaptable, resourceful nature ensures that you will never stay in a rut for long. If you find yourself in a desk job, where you are required to do certain repetitive things, you would probably jump out the nearest window—or, more likely, turn in your resignation. You need a job that has many different aspects to it, one that involves places to go and people to see, or you will become bored. Progressive, creative, clever, and innovative, you are especially well-suited to careers in marketing, advertising, and sales.

Your 5-Destiny makes it easy for you to be a team player. You do not need to be the head honcho or in the limelight, though many of you end up there because you are so well liked, efficient, and capable.

SOCIALLY

You are the consummate social participants; the all-around good guys and gals. If you belong to a social group and something needs to be done for an event or cause, you are the best people to do it. Promoters, networkers, organizers, and orchestrators—when inspired or motivated by a cause, you can sell more tickets, contact more people, sign up more volunteers, and make more things happen than anyone else.

Chameleon-like in nature, you are drawn to people of diverse cultures and backgrounds. Most of you are more liberal than conservative, but you enjoy being included in all types of social gatherings, regardless of the political or social customs and credos associated with the event.

All people who resonate to the high side of the 5 want freedom and justice for all and are the sponsors or participants in many of the most liberating causes. As an aside, the United States of America has a 5-Destiny (7/4/1776 = 7+4+1+7+7+6 = 32 and 3+2 = 5), and the name "America" also reduces to a 5 (America = 1+4+5+9+9+3+1 = 32 and 3+2 = 5), which is the number that is most associated with freedom and the freedom fighter. Some of the most colorful and, in some cases, emancipating presidents of the United States had 5-Destinies; i.e., Thomas Jefferson, Abraham Lincoln, Theodore Roosevelt, and Franklin Roosevelt.

FRIENDSHIP AND LOVE

Love is as important to 5-Destiny people as it is to just about anyone but, if you wait too long to "settle down," your desire for constant change and variety may greatly challenge your chances of finding and committing to your perfect match. Once you have committed to lifelong love, however, you can be very loyal and dedicated. It is important that you make sure your "chosen one" has an abundance of energy like you, and many of your same interests, because you are not prone to allowing anyone to clip your wings. If someone can't or won't keep up with your busy and activity-packed lifestyle, you may leave them blowing in the breeze (and a cold one at that), as the expression goes.

Diversity and change are the common threads that run through your friendships. You are not one to stay long in a relationship that starts to bore you. In fact, some of you can be quite elusive and evasive when it comes to committing to friendship as well as love relationships. It's not that you are not friendly and fun companions and acquaintances, it's just that you are so independent, restless, curious, and caught up in what's new and on the move, sometimes your friendships suffer as a consequence—but you don't—you just move on and on and on.

THE NOT-SO-GOOD NEWS
THE RESTLESS WANDERER

Because of your need for variety and constant change, some of you can become Jacks- and Jills-of-all-trades but masters of none. Those who resonate to the Restless Wanderer side of this number vibration may have rather unstable lifestyles. Your staying power is usually minimal, sometimes due to thinking there is always a better job than the one you have or even a better place to live. Or you may be continually driven to alter any static situation you find yourself in because of your gnawing need for new and different stimuli. The desire for variety can be one of the strongest contributing factors to your problems with love relationships, too.

FREEDOM OBSESSION

Freedom in every facet of your life can be so essential to you that you become very skilled at finding ways to quickly remove yourself from inhibiting and confining circumstances, even to the point of appearing, or being, irresponsible and unreliable. Once you decide to settle down, however, and conform to some of the dictates of society, most of you find a new freedom. This freedom comes from being secure and having a stable home life. A "stable and secure" life for a 5-Destiny person doesn't have to mean that you will have a sedate life, however. No way! Like Einstein once said (he was born on a 5 day), "Something's moving!"—and it's usually someone with a 5-Destiny.

INDULGENT NATURE

Many of you are also prone to overindulgences. Shop-a-holics, alcoholics, food-a-holics, and even sex-a-holics, often have a 5 as their Destiny, Personality, Character, or Attitude number. Dean Martin, Marlon Brando, Johnnie Carson, Richard Simmons, Bobby Brown, and Mick Jagger are well-known people with 5-Destinies who have had (or continue to have) over-indulgent tendencies. A strong reason for this inclination is that the 5 is the symbol of speed (ruled by Mercury). As a consequence, most people with this Destiny number have mercurial minds and postures, and many of you have a propensity for eating, drinking, talking, and driving faster than you should.

A TENDENCY TO EXAGGERATE

Being elusive and evasive, exaggerating, and downright lying are other foibles that many of you are prone to effect when resonating to the negative side of the 5. Because of your quick wit, clever use of words, and natural storytelling and sales abilities, it is sometimes very difficult for you to resist enhancing whatever catches your fancy with superlatives. However, some of you take this inclination to an extreme, getting caught in a web of your own making by telling tales that aren't that truthful and thereby making it very difficult to maintain the confidence and credibility you desire from others.

If you identify with some, or all, of the negative factors associated with the 5-Destiny, you have some work to do. It is most important for people with 5s to form good habits. Depending on your Personality or Character numbers, it may be easy for you to express the positive side of the 5, but, if you have more than one 5 in the six primary numbers of your chart, you may benefit by following the advice in the Motivational Project.

MOTIVATIONAL PROJECT

Every day make the effort to do just one extra curricular thing that is good for you. By tackling just one thing at a time, until it becomes habitual, you will help yourself to build greater stability in your day-to-day life. Sticking with one thing until it becomes a habit is the most effective way for people with 5-Destinies to overcome their most frustrating shortcomings.

DESTINY NUMBER 6

The path of the good citizen and cosmic parent to all.

THE GOOD NEWS

People with a 6-Destiny are some of the most responsible and caring humans on this planet. You are principled and patient, conscientious and careful, home-lovers and hospitable, devoted, and dedicated to your families, friends, jobs, and your favorite causes.

The dominant natural talents you possess include having an exceptional ability to teach and manage others. You are presented with many opportunities to showcase these talents (regardless of whether you are a teacher or manager by profession) because of your innate desire to help and be of service to your fellow humans. Your most spontaneous service and caretaking inclinations are inspired by your need to be needed. Because of that, you are also superlative pet owners and plant/garden tenders, and you are usually the first to volunteer to help all those that have difficulty helping themselves.

AT HOME

Comfort is your cornerstone—bringing comfort to others and feeling comfortable yourself. As a consequence, your home is usually decorated in a warm, cozy way. If you are a guy and your wife has decorated your home in a less-than-cozy manner, you will likely have a favorite chair or room in the house where you can have your comfort needs met.

Your home is definitely where your hearts lies, and you would rather be there than anywhere. In fact, many men with the 6-Destiny become "house moms," or the primary caretaker of their children, while their wives work outside the home. Both sexes with a 6-Destiny would prefer to work outside their home, if possible, regardless of what their job might be.

If you have children, they tend to be your top priority. Being gifted with wonderful patience and a natural proclivity for teaching, you can thoroughly enjoy helping your kids with their homework and learning skills. Making sure your children's essentials and incidentals are met also feeds your (sometimes all-consuming) desire to be needed.

Having pets, a garden, or many potted plants are things that most people with a 6-Destiny require in their environment because, again, you are *nothing* if you are not taking care of *something* or *someone*. It's simply your basic nature to do so and, fortunately, you are really, really good at it!

AT WORK

If you are the typical 6-Destiny person, you are as responsible and con-scientious on the job as you are in your home and community. You are the type who always goes the extra mile —- finding more things to do that you know need to be done —- even things that aren't a part of your job descrip-tion! Yes, you are the type of employee that, like the Energizer Bunny, just keeps on working away at whatever needs your attention until you render yourself entirely indispensable!

Anyone who has a boss or an employee with a 6-Destiny should con-sider themselves fortunate indeed. If you are a boss, you are very equitable and just. You are also most adept at managing people, primarily because (1) you are patient and understanding, (2) you are principled and operate on a code of ethics that ensures fairness and justice for all, (3) you want to be liked and therefore present a very pleasant, non-threatening demeanor to one and all, and (4) your counseling skills are exceptional.

As an employer or employee, you are excellent team-players. Regardless of your position, you can be very effective and comfortable in a secondary role—even a subordinated role—because most of you believe that it is best to work together as a team for the greater good.

SOCIALLY

All of you are social. You enjoy the company of family and friends and also attending community events and social gatherings. If you are a woman and you are invited to a party of a friend, you will most likely bring more than you're asked to bring in the way of food and beverages, or gifts, and/or you will stay afterward to help clean up. And, sometimes you do those things for people you don't even know!

If you are a guy, you are the type who enjoys the social company and conversation of women more than men. That's because the majority of you are lovers, not fighters! You can simply find more enjoyment talking about your children, their school and school events, gardening, pets, and even cooking, than football and buxom babes. Right? Well, some of you may enjoy the latter too but, if you really think about it, you may realize that you actually *do* prefer the girl talk.

As a guest, you are the best, because you are so considerate and conscientious about helping or, at the very least, not making more work for your host/hostess. No matter where you are, you will do something to ease the workload or to comfort others. Sounds like you're such nice folks! Actually, yes, you *are*!

FRIENDSHIP AND LOVE

There is no better or more devoted friend than someone with a 6-Destiny. Your friendships are very important to you; therefore, you nurture them on a continuous basis. You remember birth dates and orchestrate parties and other get-togethers for friends. You are very understanding and sympathetic, loving and caring, congenial and accommodating. You *want* to *help* everyone, especially your friends and family members.

As a lover and mate, you can be openly affectionate and physically demonstrative. In fact, hugging was probably invented by a 6-Destiny person. As with everything else in your life, when you are in love, you will extend yourself beyond the call of duty. You can truly be the gift that keeps on giving for your lucky mate. Most of you never receive back as much as you give, but that's mainly because no one can *ever* keep up with all your generosity, let alone get one step ahead!

THE NOT-SO-GOOD NEWS

A RESEARCH AND ANALYSIS FREAK

Some of you cannot purchase *anything* without researching every facet about whatever it is you want or need. If your mate has a more action-oriented Destiny number, this can be the source of many squabbles between the two of you. It is the author's belief, however, that your mate should appreciate the fact that most of the things you ultimately *do* purchase are quality items, usually purchased at a good price, that last forever.

PICKY, PICKY, PICKY!

Many people with a 6-Destiny go overboard about cleanliness and hygiene. Sure, it is nice when the house is spotless and there's no cat fur dangling from the couch cushion, but some of you never rest till you know that you have scrubbed your place to perfection. Eccentric Howard Hughes (born on a 6 day with a 6-Destiny) is an example of overt fastidiousness developing into a phobia and a paralyzing *fear* of germs. Take care to ensure that your love of cleanliness does not become so extreme that it becomes an obsession and/or develops into a neurosis or worse.

Another area of your life where you tend to be ultrapicky is in choosing a marriage mate. If you are the type of 6-Destiny person who seeks out people who "need to be fixed" in some way (6-Destiny people are the most prone to "co-dependent" relationships), you won't be as picky in this area, needless to say. But, if you have a strong appreciation of yourself and your giving nature, you are more than likely to be very cautious about marrying someone who would take from you without giving back. By the time you are ready to connect with a lifetime partner, you know yourself and your giving tendencies too well, and it becomes very important to you that your life partner be someone who appreciates and reciprocates in this area. Even though it may take you a longer time than many to make a marriage connection, this is not something to feel bad about. Many 6s wonder *why* they haven't found the man or woman of their dreams, and now you may have some clue.

SELF-RIGHTEOUSNESS AND MARTYRDOM

Two of the worst qualities those with 6-Destinies can exhibit are self-righteousness and being a martyr. Self-righteousness is a characteristic that is difficult for most of you to avoid because, after all, you *do* think you know what's right for *everyone* and *everything*, right? Right! Just because you think and feel so strongly about the things that are important to you (every parent should put his child's needs first, every animal should be spayed and have a loving home, etc.) doesn't mean that *everyone cares* about those things like you do. In fact, it is a difficult pill for most of you to swallow when you begin to realize that very *few* people feel the same way about things that you do. If things were perfect, most people would have 6-Destinies, and then this would be an almost-perfect world in which to live. But since things don't work that way, some of you must learn to *lighten up*, take care of your own little acre of space, and just let others be the way they are. The fact is, when you become self-righteous, you can become one of those hard-to-be-around people who want to tell everyone else what to think, feel, and do. As a consequence, many people will try their best to avoid you. At its worst, your intolerance is like a weed that can overtake all of your positive attributes. Most of you are exemplary in the way you manage your own lives, and that's a wonderful thing in itself. So set a good example for others, and perhaps you will have a profound influence on one or two people, and that's a great lifetime accomplishment!

The second most negative aspect, martyrdom, goes hand-in-hand with your inability to say NO to *anything* or *anyone*! You give and give and give and then race out to give some more, so that no one will ever think you haven't given enough! It's almost as if you're trying to overcompensate for some unfounded lack you see in yourself. And then you want everyone to *appreciate* how much you have given, even when no one has asked you to do a thing. The end result is that you set yourself up to become the martyr by your refusal to put limits on your giving and to stop doing the things that you know won't be appreciated anyway.

BEING EXCESSIVELY ARGUMENTATIVE

Your code of ethics and firmly-held principles lie at the bottom of your inability to just leave things alone. If you have been treated in an unfair way, or if you don't like the way someone spoke to you, or you're displeased with some other event or occurrence, you can argue and rag on someone until they're worn out and exasperated. It's ironic that your home is the most important thing to you and yet, many times, you are the one reason it is not the kind of place you would like it to be—a place of serenity and harmony. Your pickiness can be a basis for many an argument, too. If someone didn't put the toilet seat down, or left their hand laundry hanging all over the bathroom, or didn't vacuum the rug properly, or didn't mow the lawn just so, you can really get out of control. Picky, picky, picky. Think about it. How would you like to be on the receiving end of *you*? If you dream of a more peaceful existence, then maybe you need to make the first move. Find other ways to express your needs and preferences rather than blasting away at those you love the most.

BEING SMOTHERING

Yes, you are one of the most giving people. And, yes, you are one of the most nurturing people. But you can also be one of the most smothering people for those who live with you and love you. This comes from your need to be needed, and because of that you set people up to depend on you for everything. Even once your children are grown and ready to fly the coop, some of you are still "in their face" with your "need to be needed." The people who love you know that you are doing what you do for them out of love, but your behavior can become very bothersome once they are ready to develop their own sense of independence and autonomy. This author's suggestion is to get really involved in something. Focus on your community's needs or just go to a shelter and adopt a dog. Do whatever it takes to help you allow your children or other loved ones to cut themselves free from your apron strings or suspenders.

STUBBORNNESS

This final negative about 6-Destiny people is important to be aware of because some of you can become so set in your ways and so impossible to reason with that you can make life very unhappy for yourself and everyone in your environment. If you identify with this nature and would like to change, it is suggested that you try each day to take a different approach or give a different outlook to something about which you have already made up your mind. Is there something you would *never* change or a concept about which you would *never* agree? If you really want to change, you can but, since you are so stubborn, just being open to change may be your biggest obstacle! Just remember, once you have recognized the problem, you are halfway there. Good luck!

MOTIVATIONAL PROJECT

If you feel as though you are not getting as much out of life as you would like, then it is up to you to stop doing the things that are getting in your own way. Those of you with the 6-Destiny, more than any of the other Destiny numbers, create most of your own problems because you instinctively *know* right from wrong, good from bad, and most of you desire peace and harmony. Whether it is your need to be someone's savior or your inability to say "No," or your intolerance of others' lifestyles and viewpoints, *you* have the power to change your life to make it more what you want! Actually, *everyone* does, but because your Destiny number requires you to be responsible, conscientious, nurturing, comforting, and an exemplary citizen, YOU have all the tools and know-how to change your life for the better—and there's no better time to start than now! This author knows and has great respect for people who resonate to the positive side of this wonderful Destiny vibration. It is her opinion that the world would be a better place with more 6-Destiny people who exhibit the positive traits referred to in The Good News!

DESTINY NUMBER 7

The path of the scholar, the perfectionist, and the keeper of secrets.

THE GOOD NEWS

Dignity is the most important element of your existence. You are loath to bring unwanted attention to yourself or to make a fool out of yourself. For those reasons, most of you learn at an early age to listen rather than talk. The nice thing about being so contained is that when you do have something to say, people usually want to listen. Some 7-Destiny people are not as quiet and contained as others, but most of you rarely share much information about your personal lives.

Also, you do not appreciate meddlesome people and do not seek personal information from others—even from those closest to you (unless you are a private investigator or the like, as some of you are). You don't pry or ask about the lives of others because you don't like anyone asking you about what you consider to be your personal business. It's as simple as that.

Almost everyone with a 7-Destiny is a perfectionist in one way or another. Usually this need to do whatever you do to perfection is most evident in your work habits, which helps you to become masterful in any endeavor you choose. Most of you love to analyze and research and, even if you choose the fields of medicine or law, your favorite part of those occupations is gathering facts and analyzing your findings.

Your broad and ever-expanding interests in the sciences, the philosophies, the arts, the religions, and the mysteries of life and the world, inspire in you a lust for learning. The 7 is the number of genius, mastery, truth-seeking, individualism, ingenuity, competence, analysis, introspection, investigation, originality, telepathy, and innate wisdom. Are you impressed with yourself yet!?

AT HOME

All 7-Destiny people are very private and desire a quiet and calm environment. You may even have an alcove or room in your home where you can go to escape from the rest of the world for a while. You are happiest in familiar surroundings, doing your own thing. You may have a serious hobby, one that takes up a lot of your time, or one project after another at home that keeps you busy and away from the clatter and chatter of everyday life.

You are either extremely orderly or you lack concern for order in your home altogether. Comfort is important to you, but your idea of comfort may not conform with the norm. Your decorating tastes are usually unconventional and may lean toward the abstract and unique, with some cultural and ethnic overtones.

AT WORK

Most of your work associates probably agree that you have an exceptional mind and profound concepts and ideas. You are not someone who readily touts your expertise and ingenuity, but you prefer to keep your opinions about yourself and others to yourself. Eventually everyone who works with you becomes aware of the bevy of knowledge that is within you. And, even though many of you avoid mundane chitchat, you thoroughly enjoy participating in lively discussions or debates on topics that you know well. Co-worker conversation aside, for the most part, you like to work as autonomously and independently as possible, and when you are able to effect that kind of atmosphere for yourself, you tend to do your most brilliant work.

SOCIALLY

You are not the type who clamors to be included in the "in crowd" even though you greatly appreciate the finer aspects of the cultured life like ballet, the symphony, museums, the theater, and travel. In fact, if it weren't for your all-consuming desire to learn and constantly expand your understanding and knowledge of all of life's bounty, you might avoid a social life altogether. Men, more than women, born under this vibration, have much less motivation to go out on the town—for any reason. If they socialize at all, they prefer the company of their closest friends in familiar surroundings or in their own home. Seven-Destiny women, on the other hand, are more gregarious but, like the men, do not gravitate toward the more ostentatious aspects of society. When either sex does grace the social scene, however, you can be interesting and comely additions to any gathering.

FRIENDSHIP AND LOVE

You are attracted to unique and unusual people—no mainstream types for you! As a consequence, your love relations may be somewhat avant-garde. You are drawn to mysterious and sometimes unavailable partners because you may be like that yourself. As the old expression goes, "birds of a feather flock together," and that would be true for many of the people to whom you are attracted.

Because you are so private about your own personal life, you are attracted to others who have the same quality. You tend to be someone who has his/her own, sometimes very unique religious, philosophical, and political views and attitudes, and, due to that, you will meet and form relationships with those who walk to the beat of their very own drum, too. In fact, sometimes your personal likes and dislikes can be quite enigmatic to people who don't know you very well and also, at times, to your closest friends and family members!

Depending on the other numbers in your chart, you may or may not be very openly warm and loving. Most of you do not like public displays of affection, but you are certainly amenable to romantic rendezvous and cuddling quietly in the dark corner of a candlelit restaurant.

THE NOT-SO-GOOD NEWS
A SOUNDING BOARD

Your penchant for privacy has another consequence that most of you don't really enjoy. People are so inspired by your wonderful ability to listen so well that they tend to unload their most burning problems on you. Even though you never encourage such actions, your contained nature can appear to be like a safe haven for those who need to tell someone about their overwhelming stresses and misfortunes. They assume that you will never tell anyone else what they say, and they are quite right. In fact, you are quite capable of carrying even the most shocking information about yourself and others to your grave.

DOING THINGS YOUR WAY!

Control issues are also prevalent among 7-Destiny people. You do not like anyone telling you how to do your thing, whatever that might be. You will, however, listen politely but continue to do whatever you were doing in your very own way. You are most capable of getting any job done, and usually in a much more superlative manner than others. Your boss, friends, and family members usually know that you produce your best work when left on your own.

EXTREME PERFECTIONISM

Your need for perfection can cause you to be overly critical of some of the things those closest to you do. If your penchant is to save money, you will think everyone should save money. If you don't drink alcohol or smoke, you will feel that no one else should either, and you will make your opinions known in subtle ways. One of the ways to cure yourself of being so critical of others is to remind yourself of the many things you have not done perfectly over the years. If you are honest (which some of you have a problem being), you will admit that not everything you have done merits a big gold star!

ANTISOCIAL TENDENCIES

Some 7-Destiny people can be so secretive and disassociated from "normal" society that you come close to being wholly antisocial. Many of you follow careers that demand rigorous isolation, such as working for the

C.I.A. or being secret agents, and you can get a real thrill out of being secretive and mysterious to others. Both sexes have the ability to keep their mouths shut—becoming so adroit at using silence that you can use it to intimidate or bring down others' defenses. In your personal life, some of you can become extreme loners and even hermits if your "private" side gets carried to an extreme.

LOSSES AND FEELING YOU ARE DIFFERENT THAN OTHERS

Many of you experience grave losses at an early age that may throw you into a melancholic state for many years. A 7-Destiny sometimes creates scenarios that bring about feelings of loss or isolation, of being different, left out, and alone. These feelings can become the impetus for bringing your inherent genius and masterful abilities to the surface. Beethoven, for example (born on a 7 day with a 7-Destiny), lost his hearing and yet went on to create brilliant music.

LEADING DOUBLE LIVES

There is a very strong propensity for 7-Destiny people to carry on extracurricular affairs and relationships or to live a life that, if exposed, could possibly destroy your home life or career. This "double life" thing is not uncommon among 7-Destiny people. As mentioned previously, many of you enjoy being a mystery and especially like being involved in the clandestine. Princess Diana of England, Marylyn Monroe, President John F. Kennedy, and J. Edgar Hoover are some examples of famous 7-Destiny people whose secret lives have now been revealed.

EXTREME MOODS

Sometimes you can be very melancholy and moody because the 7 is a pensive, introspective, contemplative number that can cause you to over-analyze and become overly critical of yourself and others. Since most of you are not very social anyway, this tendency can cause you to seek addictive alternatives, like alcohol, drugs, and food, to allay your blues.

MOTIVATIONAL PROJECT

If you are feeling left out and alone, as if you don't fit in and never will, or if you are depressed and lonely most of the time, then it is time to realize your masterful calling! Having a 7-Destiny ranks you among some of the most brilliant and creative people ever—and *you* may be what's holding you back from realizing your grandest potential! No matter what your circumstances are, call a nearby college and get a college curriculum mailed out to you. Thumb through it until you find something you would like to study, and then enroll in even one class at your earliest opportunity! You must learn and expand and constantly grow in this lifetime or you can easily get dragged down by depression or feelings of restlessness knowing that there is something else you should be doing but not having a clue as to what it is. Get going now! You will be half way there when you take the first step. All 7-Destiny people are bumped out of their comfort zones at different times during their lifetimes because this is the Destiny number of constant and soulful growth.

DESTINY NUMBER 8

The path of the watchguard, the matriarch/patriarch, the judge, the producer/director, the general and the class act.

THE GOOD NEWS

No one has more savoir-faire and aplomb than someone with an 8-Destiny. You *know* how to look good, how to help others to look good, and how to make your surroundings look *sensational*! You never settle for second best where your purchases are concerned, and most of you possess an innate sixth sense with regard to what's "in," and what's going to be "in" or "out," from fashion to stock market investments (if you are interested in those things, that is). Many of your friends and others use you as a quality barometer because you exhibit the good taste and manners that most everyone wants.

You are the quintessential dreamers of grandiose dreams. You desire the biggest, the best, the highest, and the most. Your undauntable belief in yourself, and your innate and learned talents, along with your willingness to take the chances to make those dreams come true, make you believe you deserve to have more than most, and many of you do! And the nicest thing about many with an 8-Destiny is that, once you have achieved fame and fortune, you don't flaunt your wealth, become pretentious about it, or act condescending to those with less.

AT HOME

Being the king or queen of your castle goes without saying for someone with an 8-Destiny. Your surroundings usually reflect your impeccable taste and artistic style. As a mate and parent, you have your own way and manner of doing things around the home, and those who live in your environs usually adhere to your rules and requirements—or, well, heads just might roll!

From a casual picnic in the park to a gala sit-down dinner for twenty or even a beer-bust with the guys, you will orchestrate the details of any event like a captain running a tight ship. The decor must suit the occasion right down to the most minute detail. Whenever you preside over an event, everyone enjoys themselves. Whether you are male or female, you are the Martha Stewarts (another 8-Destiny person) of life because class and quality are your cornerstones.

You are disciplinarians with a soft side, too, and even though you may come across like commanding officers at home, you simply don't know how to do it another way. Growing up, you were probably the bossiest of your siblings, and you probably run your office the same way if you work out of the home. Your objective is to achieve the greatest quality and efficiency in everything you are associated with—and that includes your home, your mate, and your children.

AT WORK

From managers and executive assistants to shop owners and professionals, you were born to organize and make things run efficiently. In whatever position you find yourself, you become known for your competence and first-rate effort. As related above, it's the only way you know how to do things.

The 8 is also associated with judgment, and many of you can simply glance at someone across a room and know you don't want to have anything to do with him/her. This keen sense may have to do with your heightened intuition, but it's also because you can spot quality (or the lack thereof) instantly, from how someone acts to how well-groomed they are, and you easily ferret out even the slightest flaw. Because of this, you can be quite intimidating to those less inclined to your standards, but that's okay with you. After all, you are just staying true to yourself and your values and that's also a quality trait, right?

Many of you become judges because you are so keen on rules and regulations and interested in the laws of the land. The good thing is that, although your heart does not entirely rule your head, you do allow it to play a role in your decision-making process, and you can be very fair and just in your judgment calls. A great majority of you, in fact, take up the podium to help the indigent and disenfranchised and become champions of the underdog. When you find a law or rule that hinders rather than helps, you are the first ones to set out to get them changed for the better of all.

You are natural executives, administrators, the chairmen/women of the board, and the commanders-in-chief. A few presidents of the United States had 8-Destinies—George Washington, James Monroe, Martin Van Buren, Millard Fillmore, Ulysses S. Grant, and Lyndon Johnson. A few first ladies had 8-Destinies, too; namely, Thomas Jefferson's daughter, Martha (acting in place of her mother who died before Jefferson took office), Lou Hoover, Nancy Reagan, and the current first lady, Laura Bush.

Men with 8-Destinies, more than women (although women are making great gains in this arena) can be financial wizards. You are naturally calculating, and both sexes love to get a deal for their money. It's not that you want the cheapest thing—you don't. You look for things that either (1) hold their value or (2) are quality items at a discounted price. Numbers and figures always play a role in your life whether it's through your occupation or simply contemplating how you are going to get the things you want the most.

SOCIALLY

To say you are protocol aficionados is an understatement. You are precision-oriented, and you readily embrace the rules and regulations of society. Therefore, regardless of your income level or career endeavor, your style and polished manners give you a natural affinity for high society. Most of you enjoy hobnobbing with the upper echelon and are patrons of the finest restaurants, spas, and the most elite playgrounds for adults.

Being people-oriented, many of you like to join groups and are usually elected to chair them. Teaching and lecturing are your natural talents, and you especially enjoy lecturing on subjects that can enlighten and help others to better their journeys through life.

FRIENDSHIP AND LOVE

Your grandiosity definitely spills over into this area of your life. You can be the *most* romantic, *most* loving, generous, and deliciously exciting person on earth. Yes, romance is an area where people with 8-Destinies blossom. You are like the director *and* the star in your own movie production, and your lucky spouse/mate/partner/date can be the recipient of an Academy Award winning effort with you at the romance helm. You can be the last of the big spenders when you are trying to woo someone into your life.

As a mate, you are committed and giving, but once you settle in for the long haul, you can get a little stuffy and rigid if you are not careful. "Lighten up" are words that aptly apply to most people with an 8-Destiny, especially with regard to the home front.

Because you are naturally giving and nurturing, you are also an especially wonderful friend to have. Like most everything else you do, when you are good, you are very, very good—and that certainly is the case in friendship.

THE NOT-SO-GOOD-NEWS
THE RIGID RULES REGULATOR

Your penchant for enforcing rules and regulations can create some problems for you. Your co-workers or friends and family members may feel you are too bossy, too demanding, or too uptight. You really are, you know. You just don't understand why people won't follow the rules! And try as you might, you can't always get people to see the wonderful example you think you set for them. The fact is that all of you eventually learn that your "teacher's pet/goody two shoes/precision operator" way of doing things does not always go over as well with co-workers and friends as it does with teachers and bosses.

DEPRESSION

Another interesting problem that many 8-Destiny people face is that of being prone to depression — even major depression. You see, when circumstances beyond your control begin to occur or your big dreams and aspirations appear to be dashed, your piqued-up psyche can drop like a lead balloon. It is good for you to understand this about yourself because many of those fear-based feelings can be avoided if you practice giving yourself a reality check every once in a while. Sure, you can still have your big dreams and plans, but when feelings of hopelessness and defeat begin to creep in, or someone you respect pokes holes in your grand plans, know that you can alleviate those extreme emotional letdowns by recognizing that there are always options and alternatives to *every* plan in life. When circumstances don't seem to be going your way, you may just need to have more patience for a while or, even better, think of an alternative way to effect your plans and dreams.

WHAT GOES AROUND, COMES AROUND

It is important for you to know that when one has an 8-Destiny, you get back exactly what you give out, sometimes with shocking swiftness. You may have noticed that if you tell a little white lie, you either find yourself defending that lie or being the recipient of an obvious lie from someone else. No matter what you do, it will come back to you. If you cheat, you will be cheated upon; if you steal, you will be stolen from; and, if you do something good for someone, someone will repay your goodness and do something nice for you. This number vibration can take you to the highest of the highs or to the lowest of the lows, depending on how you decide to live it. Basically, your Destiny is higher than most; therefore, more is expected and required of you and your actions. *And,* you *know* how good you *are* when you do the right thing!

MOTIVATIONAL PROJECT

Now that you have had your talents and abilities validated and you better understand the problems that can hinder their advancement and fruition, all you have to do is get yourself out there and do the things you do so well! If you haven't come up with anything that you think deserves your full-blown attention, put your thinking cap on because you have come into this life to do great things—and you *know* that! You may choose to be a wonderful parent or a great employee, and those are excellent goals and endeavors. But most of you think in terms of *money, power, and fame!* (Oops, your secret is out!) Maybe that's because the number 8 represents money, power and fame. The 8 can bestow those things upon you, too, but there's a catch. You have to *work for* them! The extra good news is this: The harder you work and the more dedicated you are toward manifesting your goals, the more the 8 will return to you. The 8 guarantees that you will receive back what you give out, and it usually returns more than you could have ever dreamed of (well, maybe not *all* your dreams because many of them are in another dimension). You've a powerful Destiny, and you know how to do an exceptional job or exhibit your talents in an extraordinary way, so what are you waiting for—get going *now* to make your dreams become a reality!

DESTINY NUMBER 9

The path of the "old soul" and the universal humanitarian.

THE GOOD NEWS

The 9 Destiny bestows on you a natural sense of gentility and aristocracy. Even if you were brought up in a modest or low income home, most of you knew from an early age that you wanted to get something more out of life than for what most people settle. You have always been drawn to the finest things, from Cartier jewelry to BMWs, and now you know why. You are caught up in exterior appearances, and if you think you are too down-to-earth to be described this way, look around you. One or more of your favorite possessions will prove this to be true and will likely project that there is a lover of fine things lurking within you.

The 9 is called the number of the "old soul." What that means is that you have the ability to draw from and use your past life knowledge more readily than someone without a 9-Destiny. Because your innate knowledge and understanding are so accessible, you may sometimes feel that you should receive more respect from others just because you are so wise. Being an older and therefore wiser soul, your mission is to be more humane, humble, and giving than most others. As you well know, respect is earned on the earth plane through actions, accomplishments, and demeanor so, regardless of how old your soul is, you have to do what everyone else has to do to garner the kind of respect and recognition you desire.

AT HOME

Many of you tend to be conservative in your views and politics and because of that you feel you should be liked and respected by your peers, your neighbors and society. By doing the right thing, expressing the right words, wearing the right attire, living in the right neighborhood, and having your kids in the right schools, etc. you believe you are doing what you should be doing, and that others should take notice. Actually, you are usually a model citizen, unless you get carried away with your own philosophy and believe that your way is the only way. That's never a good thing, you know.

Usually 9-Destiny people have to do a lot of giving in their lives. You don't necessarily set out to do that, it's just that circumstances prevail and create situation after situation that require your attention and take up your time. You may have to take care of more children than you planned, or have one child that requires your inordinate attention, or a mate who needs much more from you than you need from him/her, and so on. Whatever the case, that is what this Destiny number is all about—giving, and to be more exact, giving *selflessly*!

Your home may or may not be a designer's dream, but it will be well-kept and comfortable. If you are fortunate enough to have the money to afford the environment you want, your tendency may be to overdo things in a showy, even garish way, rather than with elegant taste. Elvis Presley had a 9-Destiny, and most of us have seen what he did with his decor. However, being the symbol of aristocracy and gentility, many of you have an innate sense of taste and a flair for creating exquisite surroundings when you are so inclined.

AT WORK

Nine-Destiny people have a wide spectrum of occupations that they can do well, from the arts and sciences to politics and athletic endeavors. One thing is for certain, though, you must feel proud of what you do and where you work. And, if you do not feel properly respected (which is the most important thing to you), you will not enjoy your work. You need to be verbally and/or monetarily acknowledged for a job well done. You especially grow to resent your boss or co-workers, or work in general, if you are not openly appreciated. Most of you do a very good job and therefore automatically receive the kind of treatment you crave. You do not like to be told what to do, however, and the more someone works with you, the more they understand that. You have your very own way of approaching everything, from typing to mowing a lawn, and you do not appreciate anyone telling you that their way is better.

Because the 9 is such an elevated number and the 9-Destiny is required to learn selfless giving, many of you find yourselves working in and for the public. You are especially well-suited to working in areas that help to beautify the community or that involve bringing greater culture to it. As a matter of fact, your greatest assets are your pleasing public demeanor and your effective and eloquent verbal skills and, because of those assets, you can be a strong force when associated with local or national politics.

SOCIALLY

You were born to socialize! Most of you enjoy putting on your fanciest duds and having someplace to go where you'll see and be seen. Some of you are sports enthusiasts, but the vast majority of you have more sophisticated tastes, like the symphony, the opera, the ballet, and the theater. You love fine wining and dining, and your talent for being pleasing and polite makes you a popular guest and companion at any social gathering.

You are naturally drawn to charity organizations and fundraising groups, partly because they hold wonderful social events throughout the year. You like to be affiliated with organizations that are involved in philanthropy and humanitarian issues and, because of your verbal eloquence, appealing demeanor, and people-pleasing attitude, you are frequently asked to chair the committees and groups in which you become involved. Once you have achieved a degree of status, you can also become exceptionally generous philanthropists.

All of you love to travel. Once you get the travel bug, you will not be happy unless you can take an extended trip at least once or twice a year. You love the entire ambiance of travel—the new and different people, places, and things. Your basic nature is one of universality, and the more time you can spend flying around in the universe, the better you like it.

FRIENDSHIP AND LOVE

"It's just as easy to love (marry) someone who's rich as it is someone who's poor" is an adage that probably was written by someone with a 9-Destiny. In order to effect the lifestyle that you want, you have to meet and marry someone who can either match or, better yet, enhance your spending power. Most of you are not prone to marrying for love alone. Your motto might well be "survival of the finest," meaning that, one way or another, you will have the fine things you desire in this life. That is important information for your mate to understand before he/she walks down the aisle with you. Once you are in a compatible and committed relationship, however, you can expend tremendous effort yourself toward attaining the lovely life you desire — even though your preference would be to marry into it.

Some, but not all, of you can be quite demonstrative when showing affection but, since your fundamental approach to life is fairly conventional and conservative, you are always careful not to be too demonstrative in public places. You are only as romantic as you *want* to be, but, if you feel like it, you can put together the most exciting, scintillating and captivating "love" scenario imaginable. On the other hand, you might not attempt to "romance" your mate at all, thinking that he/she should simply enjoy what you like to do. This does not always serve you well since not every woman is a sports fan and not every man likes to go to the ballet. Most of you are required to compromise during the dating game because of this inclination to do only the things that you like. In this regard, you can be a bit selfish.

As with your job, you also need to feel a sense of pride in your mate. He/she will have to live up to certain criterion before you are ready to get serious. This may include how well they dress or speak, their educational background, their spending habits, their family roots, and so on. There is a bit of an elitist in you,too, you know.

THE NOT-SO-GOOD-NEWS

R-E-S-P-E-C-T

You can become downright verbally violent if you don't receive the kind of respect you feel you deserve, and this, obviously, is a negative trait. As mentioned earlier, your eloquent use of words is one of your greatest assets, but that same ability can make words your greatest weapon! The words that flow from you in an angry state are like those no one else could deliver. You go for the emotional jugular vein of your opponent. You can have a way of remembering all the past utterances and actions of your opposition that you didn't appreciate, and when you become angry with him or her, you can erupt like a volcano, spewing angry words of all those long-held irritations and frustrations. You are much less prone to erupting like this in public, but at home, your outbursts can be commonplace, and they are extremely hurtful to those who live with you. In order to soften your temper tendencies, you might think about the kinds of things you have said to people. Then put yourself in their shoes. Would you like to be yelled at and talked to the way you lash out at others? After all, your Destiny number is associated with gentility and aristocracy, so wouldn't it be in everyone's best interest for you to curtail this unattractive aspect of your nature?

DEPRESSION

Some of you do not let your frustrations vent, and because you have a temper, internalizing your anger can cause you to become depressed— sometimes severely. If you can understand that your emotions need to be dealt with—not by throwing a temper tantrum, but by expressing your pain and emotional needs—you can begin to dissolve your depression's hold on you. You may have gone for years with bottled up emotions and the need to express your feelings! A remedy this author has used is this: Find a place with a bed or something soft to beat on, where you won't disturb anyone. Then SCREAM, SHOUT and/or BEAT, PUNCH and LET IT ALL OUT!! This action is comparable to the primal scream method of release practiced during the 70s, and it's quite effective and sometimes can be fun and funny, too!

MR./MS. SOMEBODY

You are prone to thinking that you are better than others. Again, this sense of self-importance can come from the fact that most of you tend to be exceptionally bright and perceptive. However, unless you use those qualities in a humble and admirable way, you have probably found that no one really cares. Many 9-Destiny people become so snobby and arrogant that you begin to lose the respect of the people you most hope to associate with—usually those who are in the upper echelon of whatever group or circle you most admire.

OVERINDULGENT LIARS AND CHEATS

Well, perhaps you are not as bad as all that, but some of you are inclined to tell whoppers (lies) because sometimes you just want people to think you are as great as you want to be. As far as cheating, most of you are not inclined to do that unless you are over-imbibers. Alcohol has a way of making 9-Destiny people (and many others) do things they wish they hadn't. Your naturally calm and dignified demeanor goes out the window (and sometimes so do you) when you overindulge in alcoholic beverages, mainly because of a bad attitude and meanness that seems to take you over. The number 9 is ruled by the planet Mars, which is the warlike planet, so you have to be extra cautious under the influence of alcohol or any other drug.

FINDING FAULT WITH EVERYONE OTHER THAN YOURSELF

When you are not doing what you want to do in your career and, therefore, not achieving what you want, monetarily and otherwise, you can be extraordinarily critical of everyone—especially those closest to you. Since most people are the primary cause of their own suffering, you might think about your role in your problems instead of putting down others or blaming someone else for everything that goes wrong in your life.

WISHING YOU DIDN'T HAVE TO WORK

Some of you don't want to work at all. You can get a big head and think that you are too good to work in a certain position, even when you don't have the degrees to qualify for the job. In some cases, you want someone else to do the work entirely while you patter about in society, doing the things that you deem worthy of your elevated view of yourself—like spending your time golfing, or doing charity volunteer work, or making sure your children are dressed better than others, or being included in everything that matters (to you). If you have the economic means available to effect that lifestyle, that's great. However, if you do not feel as fulfilled as you think you should, it is probably because you are not using your God-given talents in the manner in which they should be used. Remember, in this lifetime you have a soulful requirement to give of yourself in a noble way.

MOTIVATIONAL PROJECT

If you are unhappy or dissatisfied with your life, think about doing something giving that is outside your normal realm of unselfish contribution. If you can see this giving "requirement" in a positive light (and many of you do), then you will be on track for a happier and more fulfilled existence. In some cases, doing something that has no reward except the good feeling it gives you, can make you the happiest of all!

Nine-Destiny people have come to the earth as very evolved spirits and you are, therefore, here on an angel-like mission. For some of you, this mission may feel burdensome and not at all what you think you want or deserve. But for those who have recognized the indescribable joy you can receive from your most selfless acts, you do not need a motivational project. You are shining stars among the masses and should be applauded and honored as such; so, go ahead, congratulate yourself! The rest of you need to get to work on doing something that brings forth the kind of joy that will bring you lasting fulfillment.

DESTINY NUMBER 11

The path of the spiritual and ministerial adviser/counselor, the peacemaker, and the illuminated public figure.

NOTE: It is important to use both methods (horizontal and vertical) of addition for determining the Destiny number given in Chapter 2. You may discover that your Destiny number reduces to a 2 with one method and to an 11 with the other. In that case, it is suggested that you read both the 2-Destiny number definitions and the definitions associated with 11-Destiny. (Most people whose Destiny number reduces to this Master number have as much affinity with qualities of the 2-Destiny as they do the 11-Destiny).

THE GOOD NEWS

This Master number Destiny vibration makes you very sensitive to your surroundings. The high-tuned 11 vibration gives you the capability to readily intuit others' actions, reactions, and motives, sometimes without even being in their presence. In fact, if you allow yourself to "tune in," your psyche can be like a radio receiver. But, regardless of whether you tune in or not, you should definitely follow your hunches and take heed of your first impressions. You will discover that a high percentage of your perceptions are right on target!

Your congenial style enables you to make and retain friends and companions for a lifetime. As a member of society, you usually feel compelled to contribute selflessly to others in some way. Overall, you are very likeable, gentle, and genteel and, for the most part, a complement to the human race!

AT HOME

Most of you crave comfort and require a calm, quiet environment. Living close to water is a feature that has an especially tranquil affect on you, but if your living circumstances don't afford you these aesthetics, you will likely surround yourself with Mother Nature—placing birdbaths in the backyard, growing flower gardens, and planting trees and shrubbery. Pets are usually a part of your comfort mode, too. Utilizing the tenets of Feng Shui, the ancient Chinese method of effecting balance and harmony in an environment, is another method that helps many of you to gain a more peaceful and placid existence.

As parents, you are warm, affectionate, encouraging, loving, and fair. You are also the parent who is the peacemaker and the one your kids know is most likely to give in to their demands and desires.

AT WORK

Whether you are a salesman/woman, a high-tech or no-tech worker, or chairman of the board, you are usually well-liked by your co-workers and bosses because of your cooperative, team-playing nature and conscientious attitude toward your job and those with whom you work. As a boss, you are sensitive to, and understanding of, your subordinates' needs and daily stresses. When someone who works with you has a problem or a difficult personal situation, you are a good sounding board and an excellent counselor capable of rendering very sound and sage advice.

Many with this Master Destiny number are in positions of importance. In fact, the 11 has played a very significant role in the office of the president of the United States. For one thing, the numbers associated with the word "president," when added together, reduce to the number 11 and, interestingly, to-date, 11 presidents have either been born on the 11th or have an 11-Destiny; namely, John Adams, John Quincy Adams, John Tyler, Franklin Pierce, Andrew Johnson, William McKinley, Calvin Coolidge, Herbert Hoover, John F. Kennedy, Ronald Reagan, and Bill Clinton.

Many 11-Destiny people, both past and present, are poets, authors, clergy, diplomats, and dignitaries and, as mentioned above, many of you are destined for an elevated position in this world. The 11 is known as the number of "illumination," and it can definitely help to "put your name in lights" or, at the very least, make your name well-known among your peers and within your community. Some of you are naturally talented in so many ways that you may become well-known in more than one arena. Omar Sharif, a renowned actor and world-famous bridge player, and Shirley Temple, a famous child actress and a world-known ambassador to the U.S., both have 11-Destinies and are examples of individuals who became famous in more than one career.

SOCIALLY

You are grand social folks! You *love* music, dancing, dining, entertaining, and being entertained! You can be like the Fred Astaires and Ginger Rogerses of the 40s when you connect with your love of classical music and ballroom dancing (which is inspired by a natural sense of rhythm). As major people pleasers and delightful social company and companions, you have no problem keeping your social roster filled. From an evening spent at the opera to a "kegger" party, you are always a welcome addition and, although you are not the boisterous type, your gracious, adaptable, and non-judgmental nature makes it easy, even for the rowdy types, to enjoy your presence.

Like those with a 2-Destiny, you love to be pampered. Spending your free time at health spas or gala hotels in luxurious settings, or partaking of all the glitter and glamour of Las Vegas, lazing about on round beds with silk sheets, and dining on the most sumptuous and generous culinary delights imaginable, are just a few of life's pleasures that draw you like a moth to a flame. It would not be an exaggeration to say that the vast majority of you are addicted to life's finest things. But you also enjoy sharing all those good things with everyone you know and love and, if you have the money, you will even share with strangers! Eleven-Destiny people are some of the most generous!

FRIENDSHIP AND LOVE

As a friend, you can be the best! Both the male and female persuasions of this Destiny number are earnestly and honestly available to aid everyone you consider dear. You can listen for hours to a friend's complaints and problems and then, when you perceive the time is right, offer just the right words to soothe their pain and angst. You are loyal, dedicated, caring, courteous, and kind. You are also the type who *always* remembers every special date of your friends and loved ones with a gift or, at the very least, a greeting card. Even men with this Destiny number have an exceptional ability to remember anniversaries, birthdays, and the dates of other sentimental occasions.

The annals of love must contain volumes of creative work by people with 11-Destinies because love is your most accessible emotion! When you are smitten, you are incredibly romantic, poetic, musical, comical, affectionate, exciting, and animated in every which way! Also, 11-Destiny people are big dreamers—daydreamers, night-dreamers and out-of-this-world dreamers! So, when you fall in love, the object of your affection becomes your dream-mate. For women, he is the "knight in shining armor." For men, she is a princess to be pampered, worshiped, and adored! No wonder most of you find your life partners at a very early age!

THE NOT-SO-GOOD NEWS

SUPER-SENSITIVITY

Many of you can become frenetic and emotionally unstrung when your life gets out of balance. Those of you with this problem have probably discovered that sitting quietly in a calm atmosphere and listening to soothing music can quickly bring you back to a state of equilibrium. It is most essential for all 11-Destiny people to have a place in their home or outside in nature where you can collect your thoughts without interferences.

DISORIENTATION

A great many of you have a problem with orientation. At times, you seemingly don't have a clue as to how you got where you are or in which direction you are headed. In fact, a few of you can get confused just backing out of your driveway! This author has known many with this Destiny number who are exceptionally educated and intelligent, but when it comes to listening to directions or being direction-oriented, they act as if they are in another dimension. This Destiny number has such a high vibratory quality that you may actually FEEL as if you are on another plane of existence some of the time.

If you have not grounded yourself through some form of meditation, your energy field can expend too much energy around you, causing you to lose your sense of orientation. Using meditation to ground your energy, or practicing some other calming method, can help to alleviate some of these tendencies.

ADDICTION AND THE ENABLER

Depending on how unstable your childhood was, some of you may become addicted to alcohol or drugs, and you may have grown up with one or more family members who had similar problems. The good news is that because you resonate to this high master vibration, you have little tolerance for addictive substances. If you do overindulge in such things, you will usually spiral downward very fast, and you are likely to seek help and rid yourselves of the problem before you become helplessly hooked.

Many of you came into this life on what this author calls "An Angel's Mission." Your Master Destiny helped you to gain compassion and empathy for others through experiencing your own difficulties in your childhood and young adult years. As a consequence, some of you choose careers as counselors and other service workers in institutions, hospitals, and treatment centers.

A more likely scenario of an 11-Destiny person is that of being a helpmate to someone else with an addiction problem. Eleven-Destiny people tend to be "enablers" more than users. An enabler is someone who, even though they believe they are trying to help someone to overcome an addiction problem, actually makes it easier for the person to continue with their addiction by covering for them or helping them out financially, rather than helping them get into a recovery program. People with 2- or 11-Destinies fall in this category frequently because of their need for people to need them.

FANATICISM

Being fanatical, power-crazed, and a religious or philosophical zealot are other ways that a very small percentage of you manifest the powerful and highly persuasive qualities of this Destiny number. Many of the SS Nazi leaders in WWII were either born on an 11 day or had 11-Destinies. This number is often equated with evangelists and con artists because you can be so eloquent with words and theatrical in your delivery. You can easily move others to your way of thinking. This is a gift that some power-hungry 11s recognize they possess, and some use it to gather up their flock of faithful followers. The vast majority of you won't even come close to the above description, but some of you can become rather fanatical about the causes you believe in or the principles you hold dear. Most of the time, this radical temperament, which is usually short-lived, only occurs when you are put on the defensive about certain of your strong beliefs.

MOTIVATIONAL PROJECT

Some of you find great gratification in a quiet, comfortable existence. You may enjoy focusing your energies on your family and home life, or you may have a hobby that is more fulfilling to you than your career. As expressed in The Good News, you also usually have plenty of friends and social engagements to keep your life interesting and exciting, if that is what you desire. However, if you don't feel fulfilled with your career and wish you could change your life for the better, one suggestion is that you begin reading books that inspire you to do something more for yourself. Take yourself to the self-help area of a bookstore and let your high-tuned intuitive powers guide your purchases. If you are spiritually inclined, ask for guidance in your purchase choices. You are like "cosmic receivers" and, as such, by using meditation or just sitting quietly in a quiet place, inspirational ideas and messages can come to you. Use that wonderful gift to your advantage!

Some of you vacillate continually about changing your life in ways that you know would make it better. Take the time to figure out definitively the *one thing* you would like to do more than any other. Even if your conclusion seems to be inaccessible because of your present circumstances, at least you finally know *one thing* that could make you truly happy. That is a giant step in the right direction. You are grand dreamers, and dreams can be like energy fuses that get your mind's motor revved up. Write down your dreams, and make them into goals! Believe in yourself! You have the Destiny number that can take you to great heights, but it's up to *you* to make the decision to *begin*!

DESTINY NUMBER 22

If your birth date can be reduced to a 22 by either method of addition presented in Chapter 2, you have the innate power available to you to effect self-mastery, accumulate wealth, and even become famous! Exceptional perceptivity, intelligence, strong moral values, and ethical principles are a few of the masterful qualities that those who have this Destiny number possess. It is not easy to live up to the high standards required of the 22 because, like the number 11, it calls for a high-minded, spiritually-oriented approach to life. It is important that its power be used for the good of mankind in a humanitarian and human fashion in order to access its highest potential. By effecting that nature, you can receive honor and acclaim during your lifetime for your philanthropic deeds and altruistic nature. Like U. S. Army Generals Colin Powell and Norman Schwarzkopf, who both have the 22-Destiny, all of you with this powerful influence can be an exemplar as individuals and in the career of your choice.

Others who have risen to the masterful calling of this Destiny are computer czar Bill Gates, talk show host Oprah Winfrey, real estate tycoon Donald Trump, Red Cross founder Clara Barton, the creators of "The Greatest Show on Earth," P.T. Barnum and James Bailey, *Playboy* entrepreneur Hugh Hefner, movie mogul Woody Allen, opera great Leontyne Price, actor Jack Nicholson, renowned scientist Robert Oppenheimer, and hundreds of Olympic winners and professional athletes, to name just a few. The common threads that run through all 22-Destiny greats are idealism, goal-orientation, tenaciousness, determination, and industriousness. Everyone with this Destiny number has the potential to achieve great success, but many lack the drive and self-discipline to reach their highest potential and, when that occurs, the Destiny characteristics are experienced as a 4. It is suggested that anyone who has a 22-Destiny read the positive and negative qualities associated with a 4-Destiny, too, because the personal motivations of those whose birth date reduces to this Master number will fluctuate between the 22 and the 4 throughout much of their lives.

THE GOOD NEWS
AT HOME

As expressed above, you can be a powerhouse in the work force or on-the-job, but when you are at home, you are not inclined to want to do much of anything. A good reason for this is because you usually expend so much energy on your job that, when you are not feeling the pressure to complete a project or meet a deadline, you don't want to even *think* about anything, let alone *do* anything but relax. However, you *do* like order in your environment and, once you have relaxed sufficiently, you will set yourself in motion, like the efficient organizer and orchestrator you are, and accomplish what needs to be done on the home front.

You are also extremely dedicated and responsible parents. Your children definitely benefit from your earnest, honest, and committed approach to life. Usually, regardless of how much responsibility you have in your career, your children's needs are your priority. You may not be as available as some parents because of your jam-packed business schedule, but when you are home, you are interested in, encouraging of, and loving to all your family members.

AT WORK

The number 22 is described in numerology as the Master Builder number. If you are working toward building an empire of some sort—whether it is a charitable foundation, a social organization, or a business—you are definitely resonating to this Destiny number's highest calling. But, regardless of whether you are a business tycoon or not, when you exhibit the strong work ethic that is inherent in this Destiny, you will be a highly valued employee, boss, and co-worker—in any occupation. You are the type of employee who will arrive earlier than others, stay later, and continue to work even after everyone else has gone home (and even on weekends), if you have work that needs to be done. You could definitely be classified as workaholics, but the primary difference between you and someone who is compulsive/obsessive about work is that you thoroughly *enjoy* working!

You are also in a class of your own when it comes to problem-solving. By utilizing the qualities of logic, order, and your exceptional creative abilities, your mind functions like a high-powered computer when you make it a goal to solve a business or personal problem. Because of this skill, many with a 22-Destiny are paid the big bucks!

Your honest, down-to-earth, and conscientious demeanor garners respect from peers and colleagues alike, even though you thoroughly enjoy challenging them to fierce debates (you are great fact collectors) and occasionally you have a tendency to deliver your thoughts, ideas, and judgments in a very straightforward, sometimes disarming manner. You also have a penchant for always being punctual, especially at work, and you can be like the "Rock of Gibraltar" when you make a commitment. As an employee, you are the type who is rarely paid what you are worth because of your extraordinary dedication and responsibility on the job and your willingness to do more than you are asked. It's about time you were given some appreciation!

SOCIALLY

Most of you enjoy a full social life and are attracted to many cultural endeavors, but you are not social climbers, nor do you care about being a member of the social set. In fact, rarely, if ever, will you attend social events or gatherings where you might be required to mix with pretentious people or engage in superficial cocktail conversation. Even though you can be as sophisticated and genteel as the next person, high society is usually just not your cup of tea. Your favorite social companions tend to be good friends who share your values and tastes, and you enjoy entertaining them in your home.

When you give yourself time off from your rigorous work schedule, travel can be one of your favorite activities, and many of you see a good deal of the world in your lifetime. You don't, however, like all the fuss and bother that goes along with making travel reservations and hotel accommodations, transporting your luggage, and arranging for it to get from one place to another. Because of this, you usually find others to take care of those things for you. Whether you are a young or more mature traveler, cruise lines are well-suited to your traveling preferences since they take care of all your wants and needs.

FRIENDSHIP AND LOVE

As dynamic as you can be in your career, you can be equally exuberant as a romantic. Because 22 is a "giver" Destiny number, whether you are a man or a woman, you really *like* to give, to be helpful, and to feel needed. In fact, you can be a soft touch for anyone who is looking for a caretaker. One of the reasons you are such generous people is because you work so hard! When you have time off, and your pockets are filled with the fruits of your good efforts, you thoroughly enjoy treating those who are fortunate enough to be in your company. Most of you have few needs or expectations for yourself, so your companions can easily bask in your generosity. However, you pay attention to whether someone is reciprocating or not, and you *do* like *fairness*. When fairness and common consideration (qualities most 22-Destiny people possess in abundance) are lacking in others over the long haul, many of you have been known to end a relationship quite abruptly.

Twenty-two-Destiny women tend to leave little time for the domestic scene (cooking, baking, cleaning, etc.), mainly because it's not your favorite part of life. However, when you fall in love, you can put Wolfgang Puck and a poet laureate to shame! Your industriousness, when mixed with L-O-V-E, can turn you into an Aphrodite-like creature who can whip up prize-winning culinary concoctions while reciting your very own poetic masterpieces. Twenty-two-Destiny men want to set the world at the feet of their love interest. They are as generous and romantically masterful as their female counterparts; however, because work tends to be their priority, many of them can miss out on love altogether. So (listen up women), when they do find someone to share their lives with, they are usually quite grateful, devoted, and content within that one love relationship—for life!

This Destiny number vibration is so masterful that when you are inspired to do so, you can use its superlative qualities in any area of your life to manifest the very best of everything, even love.

THE NOT-SO-GOOD-NEWS

PESSIMISM AND STUBBORNNESS

When you resonate to the negative side of this powerful and dynamic vibration, you can be pessimistic, critical, cynical, discontent, and skeptical of everything and everyone in your atmosphere, and extremely stubborn and rigid with regard to your principles and ideals. You may automatically say "no" to every invitation or to suggestions that are offered to you, just because you don't want *anyone* disturbing your normal routine or coaxing you out of your comfort zone. If you identify with this "stuffed-shirt" kind of nature, it may be time for you to overhaul your attitude. Usually, when someone is critical of others and cynical about life, it is because he/she is not very happy with his/her *own* life and that, my friend, is *your* problem. You are the only one who can make your world better.

LACK OF SELF-CONFIDENCE AND DEFEATISM

Even though you are usually a high achiever, many of you lack self-confidence. This is not a bad thing entirely because it can make you more humble than most people, which many with this spiritual Destiny number may be inclined to be. However, lacking self-confidence can *also* make it more difficult for you to live up to the potential of your Destiny. In fact, you can get so caught up in the minor details of life that you defeat yourself over and over again by continually contemplating the ramifications of making a change or a move for the better. It is the author's suggestion that you reread The Good News, recognize that you have the same qualities and potential as anyone with this Destiny number, and realize it's about time you started recognizing your superior abilities and doing something about them! Otherwise, you will begin to live the 22-Destiny as a 4-Destiny, which is not a bad thing but basically means that you're not living up to your full potential. (See page 26 for definition of the 4-Destiny.)

LACK OF FOCUS

Most of you are very detail-oriented, but sometimes that can play against achieving your goals. You can get so caught in your own mire that you fail to see the proverbial forest for the trees. You can pass up one opportunity after another and miss out on the high level of achievement you have come into this life to experience. And there are a few of you who can even seem rather "air-heady" at times. The 22 in the Tarot is the number of "the Fool" and as such, it means that anyone who has the 22 attached to them in a significant way (as do those with a 22-Destiny) spends little time planning for the future and doesn't put much effort into learning from past mistakes. He/she lives in the moment and, as a consequence, continually falls back into the same quandary, rut, or predicament that he/she should have avoided, based on past experiences. Or, on the other hand, they are never prepared for what is right on the horizon, sometimes staring them in the face—like a financial disaster or a personal setback. If you identify with this nature, take the time each day (or once a week) to focus on one thing until it is completed. That is the best way to harness your energy force and accomplish, rather than demolish, your goals.

THE RENEGADE

Some of you take your time settling down and getting serious about your life and future. There's a strong and lively renegade that lurks within you, and if it's allowed to prevail (especially in your teens and 20s), it may take you well into your 30s before you stop trying to prove to everyone that you don't need to follow anyone else's rules to get along in life. Stubborn is not a strong enough adjective to describe your bullheadedness. You just cannot accept advice about *anything*—especially in your youth! You *must* experience everything yourself—no matter how many others may have been hurt or failed doing the same thing. You will not be satisfied until you have done whatever it is that you have set your mind to do! As a consequence, those of you who succumb to this attitude are destined to experience a rather unsavory existence for a period of time. But, if you survive your proclivities for extremes and excesses, you may eventually find yourself helping others to avoid the same pitfalls you experienced.

THE DIDACTIC AUTHORITARIAN

A handful of you can become overwrought with your sense of power and position, whether you are simply the head of the household or you feel you need to control every situation in which you find yourself. Those of you who use the power of the 22 in a negative way—to control, manipulate, or rule others—are definitely resonating to the underbelly of this high spiritual number. Anyone with this affliction would not likely be reading this book because he/she would believe they have all the answers and certainly have no desire to spend their time reading about a metaphysical science! When certain people express such negative dispositions, it is likely they experienced some very difficult and even hurtful times in their lives and did not learn the lesson of humility. Instead, they became bitter and resentful, thereby deciding to take their own woes out on everyone around them. If you identify with this character, perhaps it would be a good thing to ask yourself *why* you need to feel superior and dominate others. That type of character is usually depicted as the villain in most theatrical productions, you know. Think about it.

THE CON ARTIST OR "BLACK ARTS" DEALER

Being a con or dealing in the "black arts," such as witchcraft and sorcery, are other strong leanings of those who gravitate to the low side of the 22-Destiny. If someone with a 22-Destiny is not ready to literally "see the light" and prefers instead to wallow in the dubious and detrimental elements of the occult, his/her power can be as mighty ministering to the black arts as it can be when gravitating to a spiritual or higher calling. To this, the author would say, be mindful of the laws of the universe that offer, "What you will sow, so shall you reap." Your actions can play a significant role in how unfulfilled and unhappy your life is, or vice versa!

MOTIVATIONAL PROJECT

Throughout the above material, you will find suggestions for ways to overcome your self-limiting tendencies. They can help you realize that you are someone who, like so many famous 22-Destiny people, can be better than the best if you use the fine qualities that are inherent in you. You may not feel the need to become the next Donald Trump, Bill Gates, or Oprah Winfrey, but if you want to live by the force of the 22 (as opposed to reducing its vibration to the 4), you must do something in this lifetime that helps many people. That can occur simply by joining the Big Brothers or Big Sisters, or doing charity work at your church. Or, it can be as far-reaching as working for an international humanitarian foundation or charity.

The majority of 22-Destiny people develop an inherent desire to help others. However, with this turbocharged vibration, the mission should be to help as *many* people as possible, along with building your own character to an admirable state. May the Force be with you!

Chapter 4

The Personality Numbers

A Look at the Private You
(The Day of the Month You Were Born)

This number vibration beats to the drum of the real, "behind-the-scenes" personality. As you learned in Chapter 2, the Character, Soul Urge, and Hidden Agenda numbers express the personality qualities you show to the outside world; i.e., at the office, at social gatherings, meeting people for the first time, etc. The Personality number defines who you are in your *inside* world—at home, with intimate friends and family members.

Figuring out your Personality number is very simple. It's simply the day of the month (1st through 31st) on which you were born. Below you will find personality definitions for each day of the month. As you will see, there are some positive and some negative traits to each number at the end of each definition. The positive traits are generally some of the very best qualities exhibited by those born on a specific day. The negative traits are obviously some of the worst characteristics associated with that day's number personality. No reader will identify with every positive or negative trait.

My Personality Number Is: _____

THE PERSONALITY NUMBER DESCRIPTIONS FOLLOW:

IF YOU WERE BORN ON THE 1ST OF ANY MONTH

You are dynamic, strong-willed, and a natural leader. Your exceptional executive and organizational abilities are complemented by your innovative and risk-taking tendencies. Self-reliant and self-confident, you find it difficult to take orders from others or to be in a subordinated position. Your competitive, ambitious nature is, however, tempered by a delightful sense of humor and an awesome charm.

Whether you are male or female, you have a strong creative nature and a stylish flair. The unique style of clothing and accessories you wear, and/or the artistic interior decoration and design of your home, are obvious expressions of your innate gifts. Wearing the latest fashions and most up-to-date trends are ways you showcase your individualism. Your sense of style is yours alone, yet it is as tasteful as it is original.

Your political and philosophical beliefs can be an outlet for the practical, pragmatic you, but your dreams and personal aspirations tend to be more idealistic. You stay abreast of the latest news and events, and your penchant for collecting facts and statistics about everything that interests you makes you a very engaging conversationalist on the social scene.

Although you have a sensitive temperament and you greatly appreciate praise, encouragement, and sympathy from others, you may have difficulty expressing those same feelings of support to those you care about the most. You value tradition and the family unit, but your independent personality makes it difficult for you to surrender your personal freedom to another. When you fall in love, it is deep and abiding, and you can be a very devoted mate. You are not, however, the type to ever be dominated or controlled—by anyone!

At your *best*, you are ambitious, self-motivated, enterprising, adventuresome, independent, compelling, courageous, energetic, progressive, and charming!

At your *worst*, you *might* be selfish, domineering, begrudging, opinionated, egotistical, antagonizing, and/or lazy.

IF YOU WERE BORN ON THE 2ND OF ANY MONTH

Your generous, helpful, and capable nature makes you an indispensable "right-hand" for anyone with whom you work or live. You have the ability to understand both sides of any issue and are therefore a good arbitrator; however, on occasion you may have difficulty making small decisions when

presented with too many choices. Your exceptional ability to solve problems and provide counsel to others is enhanced by your remarkable insight
and uncanny intuition.

Although you rarely seek center stage, your quick wit and good sense of
timing enable you to deliver a commanding performance if called upon to
lecture or entertain. Your love of music and talent for dancing come from
a natural sense of rhythm. Your need to nurture inspires your love of cooking and baking, and you really enjoy having others experience your talents
by feasting on and savoring your sumptuous concoctions.

Whether you are hosting a party in someone's honor, or simply sending a
cheerful greeting through the mail, your thoughtful, sentimental disposition
ensures that you will always remember those you care about on their special
days. Collecting mementos and memorabilia may be one of your favorite hobbies, along with amassing volumes of pictures from get-togethers with family
and friends.

You are a romantic, and you can be an attentive, caring companion and
mate. You crave affection and have a strong tendency to want to get along
with everyone. At times, however, you may feel unappreciated if you do
not receive a little recognition for the myriad of things you do for those you
love, but you do not require constant accolades or need to have your ego
boosted. A simple "thank you" or an occasional gift or greeting card is what
you appreciate most!

At your *best*, you are affable, cooperative, persuasive, modest, loyal,
patient, supportive, sympathetic, trustworthy, and downright sexy!

At your *worst*, you *might* be over-sensitive, weak-willed, complaining,
self-conscious, timid, and/or a busybody.

IF YOU WERE BORN ON THE 3RD OF ANY MONTH

You have a vivid and creative imagination and can be a talented story-
teller and entertainer. You like people, and your natural charm wins you
many admirers and lots of friends of both sexes. You are rarely alone in your
pursuit of fun and creative undertakings, and you love to get everyone
together without a lot of planning ahead. Your appearance is very important to you, and you may take great pains to select just the right wardrobe

to ensure you always look your best. You may also spend hours every day exercising and choose to eat only the most nutritional foods to maintain your body in the best health and shape possible.

You can be very ambitious, and if you are inspired by a project or idea, your enthusiasm is limitless. When intellectually or creatively stimulated, you can be a moving force that makes things happen! No matter what circumstances prevail in your life, you tend to look on the positive side of everything. You are a natural networker, and when you have learned something that can benefit others, you delight in passing it on. Your adventuresome nature and zest for life are an inspiration to everyone, and you will retain your youthful attitude and vitality all your life. Your trademark glib wit and bold repartee delight all who get to know you. You may also occasionally use your superior talent with words as a very effective combative and argumentative tool.

Although you can be very romantic and openly affectionate, you can also be very picky when it comes to choosing your lifetime mate. When you finally find and marry Mr. or Ms. Right, you are a faithful and dedicated partner and, as a lover, you can conjure up the most exciting and fun-filled love sessions imaginable! You enjoy children and vice versa and, even as you grow older, the child within you readily kicks in at entertainment parks and the like, making you as excited and fun-loving as any youthful companion. As a parent, it is important to you that your children are well-behaved and responsible. As a consequence, you can be a strong disciplinarian, but very loving at the same time.

At your *best*, you are optimistic, self-expressive, good-natured, gregarious, romantic, artistic, exhibit good taste, disciplined, inspirational, and definitely foxy!

At your *worst*, you *might* be self-centered, excessively vain, too talkative, extravagant, intolerant, superficial, and/or a gossip.

IF YOU WERE BORN ON THE 4TH OF ANY MONTH

You are the proverbial "Rock of Gibraltar," and your word is as good as gold! You are a dedicated, tireless worker and are extremely good with details. Your organized mind dislikes change, clutter, and inconsistency.

You have strong opinions, and your love of debate and discussion are empowered by your excellent memory and penchant for collecting vast amounts of statistics, facts, and information.

Although you are patriotic and law-abiding, you dislike being told what, how, why, or when to do anything! Since you can be somewhat set in your ways and prone to overwork, you need to allow more time for fun and pleasure. Having money in the bank is essential to your sense of security and once you have it, you are usually practical and thrifty about your spending.

You love your home and work hard and diligently to build a solid and safe environment for yourself and your family. Puttering around the house, or staying at home and doing next to nothing, are a couple of your favorite ways to spend your free time. Despite that tendency, you will go out of your way to do favors for your friends and family and, as a conscientious citizen, you can always be relied upon to give your time to any community project you feel needs your assistance.

You have an extremely loving nature, and you possess an instinctive drive to be giving and comforting. No one can be a more dedicated, loyal, and responsible mate and parent than you. In your love relationships, you might be described as "the cog that turns the wheel" because you are so committed and feel so responsible for them. You are a traditionalist, and you hold your personal honor to the highest standards.

At your *best*, you are noble-minded, determined, skillful, ethical, cool-headed, thrifty, patient, devoted, dutiful, very honest, and totally irresistible!

At your *worst*, you *might* be unimaginative, unadaptable, stubborn, argumentative, stingy and/or somewhat crude.

IF YOU WERE BORN ON THE 5TH OF ANY MONTH

Your intelligent, enthusiastic, and genial personality makes it easy for you to inspire and motivate others. You are a natural salesperson. You have an affinity with words, whether spoken or written, and are a virtual storehouse of information and knowledge. Your progressive, curious, and investigative mind soaks up the latest news, and you are always looking for something new to try. Freedom of action, speech, and thought are essential to your desired way of life and well-being.

You are attracted to the cosmopolitan lifestyle and are frequently found among the arty set, always abreast of the latest styles and fashion trends. Brimming with energy and versatility, you are someone who can juggle more than one thing or career at one time. You do almost everything—thinking, eating, drinking, driving, talking, shopping—faster than anyone else. Impatience with details and routine matters, and being overindulgent in the pleasures of the senses, can be your greatest challenges.

Although you are a very sensual being, you seek intellectual rapport over physical appeal in a long-term mate. You enjoy mental jousting with almost anyone who is astute enough to challenge you. You are a broad-minded (albeit protective) parent and usually offer your children various challenges and adventures from which to learn.

At your *best*, you are amicable, clever, versatile, progressive, adventure-some, resourceful, a non-conformist, highly energetic, innovative, broad-minded, and utterly enchanting!

At your *worst*, you *might* be a chronic malcontent, impatient, restless, impulsive, critical of others, and/or temperamental.

IF YOU WERE BORN ON THE 6TH OF ANY MONTH

You are a lover of nature and home. Beauty is also important to you, and you have a knack for making almost any environment more appealing and livable, whether by interior decorating or landscaping. Your responsible, conscientious, people-oriented nature is a plus in any line of work that involves serving or meeting the general public. A superb host/hostess, you enjoy mixing and mingling, and the more the merrier! As such, you are also masterful at ensuring that everyone is comfortable and has a good time.

You tend to be very sensitive to criticism or admonishment and, if your ethical standards or sense of fairness and justice are questioned, you will aggressively defend your position or readily express your disapproval. Your values and principles are solidly formed at an early age, and learning to tolerate others' beliefs, attitudes, and lifestyles can sometimes be a major challenge for you.

You are very sentimental and romantic and, therefore, love, marriage, and social approval are necessary elements for your personal well-being.

You are a devoted parent, and all children have a special place in your heart. Family pets also fare very well under your cozy and comforting care. You are usually the governing influence in your home and derive great personal satisfaction from the successes of your family members.

At your *best*, you are honest, amiable, nurturing, a humanitarian, artistic, generous, caring, stable, self-sacrificing, hospitable, and physically alluring!

At your *worst*, you *might* be excessively argumentative and critical of others, stubborn, a martyr, and/or wholly self-righteous.

IF YOU WERE BORN ON THE 7TH OF ANY MONTH

You are analytical and research-oriented, and your quest for knowledge is vast and unquenchable. Strongly independent, reserved, and uniquely original, you can be somewhat difficult to get to know. Your views of life tend to be broad and abstract—liberal in some ways and conservative in others. A relentless perfectionist, you possess masterful abilities when you set your focus on your profession or toward a creative endeavor; 7s dislike taking orders from others and do better when they work alone.

Your psychic abilities are high-tuned. You can easily intuit others' moods and motives, so if you have a hunch, go with it. You are protective about your personal life and very selective about your companions; but once a friendship has been formed, it is usually a lifelong bond. Your unique personality can be highly communicative at times, especially if the subject matter interests you, or aloof and detached, with a tendency to avoid socializing altogether.

You enjoy being close to nature and, whether you are an urban or country dweller, you need a special place to go to experience quiet and calm surroundings. In fact, your need for space and the freedom to pursue your interests can create separations from your loved ones. However, once you have made the marriage/family commitment, you are a devoted mate and a conscientious, responsible, and loving parent.

At your *best*, you are wise, a visionary, patient, discriminating, dexterous, efficient, exacting, dignified, reserved, scholarly, psychic, broad-minded, a truth seeker, and very sexy!

At your *worst*, you *might* be sarcastic, overly suspicious and cynical, excessively secretive, withdrawn, passive-aggressive, inflexible, and/or slow.

IF YOU WERE BORN ON THE 8TH OF ANY MONTH

You are a born executive with a penchant for protocol. Like a general in the military or a stage director, you can be masterful at relegating and delegating. You like to gamble with life, occasionally taking wild chances and seldom taking advice. You are a dreamer of grandiose dreams, and you can make them happen! Your desire to be at the top is complemented by your keen sense of judgment, unbridled determination, and unabashed self-confidence. Your strong ambition and consistent hard work are the attributes that ensure your success!

You know the value of money, and your talent for getting the best deal is aided by your calculating mind and a desire for quality over quantity. You possess a "buyer's eye" and can become a connoisseur of the arts and artifacts. Fond of pomp and circumstance, you have a wonderful ability to create unique and outstanding events and initiate social get-togethers.

Although you are somewhat hard-nosed in your political and philosophical views, you can be a champion for the underdog. Your favorite friends tend to be like you and usually share your same views.

On the home front, your surroundings are a reflection of your fine taste and highly organized nature, even if you have to hire someone else to make it that way; grappling with household chores is not your favorite thing to do. You are selective about your mate because you want only the best for yourself. As a mate and parent, you will devote yourself to providing your family with everything it needs, and then some.

At your *best*, you are principled, refined, tactful, tasteful, a leader, a skilled manager/executive, enterprising, far sighted, a discerning judge, self-confident, powerful, and absolutely fascinating!

At your *worst*, you *might* be oppressive, intolerant, avaricious, foolish with money, rigid, scheming, selfish, unsympathetic, and/or use your power in an abusive manner.

IF YOU WERE BORN ON THE 9TH OF ANY MONTH

You are the proverbial "old soul," possessing the ability to easily access your reservoir of innate knowledge. Your heightened awareness of life and your humanitarian nature accord you great compassion and understanding for all mankind. Multi-talented, creative, and competent, you can be a leader in business or the arts. You prefer working unsupervised and do not respond well to taking orders or criticism from others.

Your material tastes are sophisticated and your interests far-reaching. Politically, you are usually conservative and resolute. Traveling and experiencing a broad range of cultural and social activities are essential to your sense of well-being, and your collection of friends tends to be just as varied and diverse.

Love, affection, and marriage are high priorities for you, but your desire for independence is equally important. In fact, you may occasionally find yourself in difficult situations at home because of your strong will and impulsive actions. However, your skillful use of words is one of your greatest assets (as well as your greatest weapon), and you can talk your way out of almost anything.

As a parent, you tend to be strong and commanding, and you don't hesitate to assign rules and responsibilities to your children. However, when your children tap into your soft side, they usually manage to find ways around the disciplinarian in you, and they get you to temper your rules in a way that benefits all of you.

At your *best*, you are helpful, impartial, generous, modest, responsible, enlightened, highly intelligent, unselfish, scrupulous, creative, idealistic, forgiving, philanthropic, loving, and absolutely charming!

At your *worst*, you *might* be self-consumed, super-critical of others, brooding, hot-tempered, and self-pitying.

IF YOU WERE BORN ON THE 10TH OF ANY MONTH

You are well-suited to operating your own business or managing one for someone else. Self-sufficient and responsible toward others, there may be many people in your life who depend on you. Your optimistic attitude will find the positive side in any situation, but your critical eye tends to always see a need for improvement. Your political and philosophical views are usually broad and open-minded. You tend to be sensible and practical most of the time, but occasionally you get caught up in some rather idealistic dreams and schemes. It's the sensitive, intuitive side of you that inspires the creativity and ingenuity that make your dreams come true!

You attract loyal, responsible friends, like yourself, but because of your strong, take-charge nature, you may have difficulty allowing your friends or family members to help you when you are in need. You especially enjoy friends whose philosophies, beliefs, backgrounds, and interests differ from yours, and your intellectual side takes pleasure in a friendly, albeit sometimes intense, debate on occasion.

Your action-oriented personality doesn't find much to like about the domestic scene, but you can excel in the culinary arts (if cooking interests you). You won't get much of a thrill out of the cleanup afterwards, however. Once you have made a marriage/family commitment, you are among the most supportive, conscientious, and devoted parents and mates. You tend to be pragmatic in your romantic life, preferring to do things that add to your knowledge—like visiting museums or attending lectures—rather than seeking pleasure and fun. Gift-giving is another area where your practicality prevails, and you are prone to give your mate something that is utilitarian rather than frivolous or fancy.

At your *best*, you are original, creative, spiritual, independent, inventive, adventuresome, ambitious, compelling, spirited, determined, persistent, self-sufficient, a good leader, and very enticing!

At your *worst*, you *might* be antagonistic, stubborn, didactic, domineering, hypersensitive, and/or controlling.

IF YOU WERE BORN ON THE 11TH OF ANY MONTH

You possess extraordinary sensitivity, brilliance, and star potential! You like the limelight and can prosper from it by using your abundance of original and creative talent. However, you must guard against a tendency to vacillate from your goals. Your outward calm and air of bravado camouflage a high-strung, nervous nature that can occasionally be moved to emotional extremes.

Although you exhibit a conservative nature, there is a rebel in you that will take an unyielding stand for an unpopular cause or belief, but this is only part of your dual nature. At times, you are cooperative and caring, and at other times, you may exhibit a selfish, rash demeanor that is entirely focused on your own needs. However, this all-consuming ego, drive, and energy definitely help you to successfully accomplish your highest goals.

Personal relationships and a sense of belonging are important to you and, although you are friendly and very charming, you are not an open book—even in your most intimate relationships. You enjoy the role of parent and provider but tend to be a bit overprotective. Your idealistic nature seeks the perfect mate, but you should be aware that what is most important is that you find a mate who can adapt to *your* unique and dynamic personality.

At your *best*, you are considerate, modest, gracious, cooperative, spiritual, outgoing, helpful, tolerant, devoted, highly perceptive, sensitive, inspiring, and super-sensual!

At your *worst*, you *might* be insensitive, miserly, condescending, vacillating and non-committal, dogmatic, and/or unrealistic.

IF YOU WERE BORN ON THE 12TH OF ANY MONTH

Your charming, clever, and good-natured personality is highly companionable, and you are sought after as a social partner and guest. Self-expression is a must for you, and you can be a talented writer, lecturer, and teacher. Your abundant imagination and gift of creativity make you a natural in the field of the arts. Doing for others gives you a warm, fuzzy feeling, and you may therefore experience a strong desire to work in the health and holistic sciences.

You tend to attract strong, individualistic friends who enjoy your easygoing, independent nature. Your desire for constant intellectual stimulation and increased knowledge motivates you to collect vast amounts of information from historical, philosophical, and scientific sources. With such all-encompassing interests, you, more than others, need to set specific goals to keep your focus and energies from becoming scattered in too many directions.

You enjoy children and they like you, too, which makes it easy for you to be a good parent. Your entertaining, fun-loving nature is well received by the younger set, as well as your friends and mate. In marriage and as a friend, you will sacrifice your own needs and desires in order to make life as good as it can be for all those you call "family"—many of whom may not even be related to you. In fact, some of you may spend a large portion of your time being caretakers, which just goes with the 12 turf.

At your *best*, you are witty, articulate, artistic, inspired, inspirational, adventurous, charming, stylish, discriminating, disciplined, optimistic, forever young, and pleasantly inviting!

At your *worst*, you *might* be excessively vain, gossipy, overly opinionated, self-centered, lackadaisical, and/or express an erratic temperament.

IF YOU WERE BORN ON THE 13TH OF ANY MONTH

You are independent, creative, and down-to-earth. You possess a strong will and great fortitude and, when involved in an athletic endeavor or pursuing a goal, your tenacity and endurance are extraordinary. You are a dedicated worker and derive much gratification from your career. Your practical, orderly nature is well-suited to any profession that calls for logic and organization. An affinity for details, numbers, and figures helps you to manage your money well and to take calculated risks that unusually pay off.

A loyal and devoted friend, your word is as good as gold, and you always come through for a friend in need. You enjoy collecting facts and debating current and historical issues with friends and family. Although you can sometimes be a bit lazy, you are happiest when mentally or physically engrossed in your favorite hobby or intellectual pursuit.

A happy home life is essential to your well-being, and you have a strong love nature; however, it may be hard for you to express your affectional and emotional needs. Your greatest challenge is an inclination to get stuck in a rut, <u>both</u> emotionally and physically. Your practical, dedicated, and conscientious nature sets a good example for your children and gives them a strong sense of security and confidence.

At your *best*, you are ethical, committed, methodical, honest, patient, loyal, moral, dependable, stable, conscientious, informative, and super sexy!

At your *worst*, you *might* be narrow-minded, opinionated, even fanatical, unimaginative, lethargic, discourteous, dogmatic, dull, and/or pigheaded.

IF YOU WERE BORN ON THE 14TH OF ANY MONTH

You are a storehouse of energy with a steel-trap mind that constantly churns out new ideas and opinions. A powerful, charismatic communicator, you speak your mind in a forthright, honest fashion, which can sometimes be a bit too candid for those doing the listening. Yours is a dual nature—logical and yet creative, responsible but elusive, intellectual but down-to-earth, law-abiding and dutiful—but always rigorously demanding of your personal freedom.

Variety is the spice of your life, and your greatest challenge is moderation, especially with temptations that appeal to the senses. Impatient and aggressive at times, you are at your best when you are running your own business and managing your own affairs. You can be lucky when gambling or risking money in a venture that's based on your own talents or achievements. You enjoy working, are a good organizer, and always honor your commitments. You also possess pronounced creative abilities that sometimes find their greatest expression outside of the workplace.

You are devoted to your family and a small, select group of friends and, although you can easily adapt to and enjoy an array of people, places, and things, you are very protective of your privacy, intimate environment, and long-term relationships. As a parent, you are conscientious and flexible in regard to your children's individual needs.

At your *best*, you are progressive, innovative, charming, daring, investigative, broad-minded, free-thinking, perceptive, productive, unconventional, sociable, and absolutely irresistible!

At your *worst*, you *might* be devious, sarcastic, super critical of others, a spendthrift, unpredictable, thrill-seeking, moody, and/or unreliable.

IF YOU WERE BORN ON THE 15TH OF ANY MONTH

You are highly independent and attracted to a variety of people, places, and things. Your creative, scientific mind craves knowledge of every kind. You also possess a good understanding of business and the world of commerce. You have a profound sense of fairness and justice but must guard against becoming a martyr or acting self-righteous or intolerant of those who don't agree with your values and ethics. You dislike confrontation and unpleasant situations, and you are adept at using your natural charm and social magnetism to easily and skillfully avoid them.

You are selective about your friends but tend to be generous and charitable to those in your inner circle. If politically or emotionally moved, you can become a most ardent and dedicated champion of a community cause. Your hobbies or recreational preferences usually involve reading, music, and the performing arts; and you can be a masterful athlete, if properly inspired.

You possess a strong sense of responsibility to your home, family, and community. As a parent, you are capable of great self-sacrifice, and you are genuine and demonstrative with your feelings of love, compassion, and caring.

At your *best*, you are responsible, accommodating, charitable, honest, unselfish, sociable, virtuous, dependable, devoted, sharing, caring, a humanitarian, and extremely desirable!

At your *worst*, you *might* be obstinate, tactless, stifling, unforgiving, picky, and/or underhanded.

IF YOU WERE BORN ON THE 16TH OF ANY MONTH

You are curious, contemplative, and introspective and require much alone time to sort through and analyze your mind's constant flow of inspiration and observation. You tend to be highly psychic and enjoy the clandestine and mystical aspects of life. Your aloof, sometimes unapproachable manner and strong need for independence, give you a mysterious allure. Although you tend to have a nervous, somewhat serious nature, you also possess an unconstrained ability to laugh, which can help you to lighten up and not be so hard on yourself and others.

You can be a procrastinator, but you are also a perfectionist and can become frustrated if you begin to feel that you aren't living up to your own high standards. You tend to place great importance on your physical appearance and must guard against allowing vanity to rule your life.

You may have only one or two very close friends, but your friendships will be enduring ones and will often last a lifetime. Family relationships mean a lot to you, but you have a difficult time expressing your emotional needs. You can become irritable, moody, and even depressed if those you love let you down. The privacy and security of your home are very important to you, and spending time in nature is very comforting and physically rejuvenating to you.

At your *best*, you are keenly observant, discriminating, dignified, confident, meticulous, patient, astute, logical, cooperative, enlightened, and immensely captivating!

At your *worst*, you *might* be standoffish, untrusting, unusual in you manner or dress, calculating, antisocial, unfeeling, suppressive, and/or stubborn.

IF YOU WERE BORN ON THE 17TH OF ANY MONTH

You are intelligent, ambitious, courageous, and possess enough energy and vitality to run a country! Common sense and an exacting perceptivity are qualities that enable you to remain calm under the most difficult conditions. You are, however, somewhat set in your ways and can find it difficult to yield to opinions and concepts that differ from your own.

You are not afraid to take chances, and with your unusual strength and originality, you can accomplish almost anything you want. Your creative talents can bring you vast monetary reward and perhaps recognition as well. You have a natural "buyer's eye," and quality is your maxim. A duality in your nature enables you to handle money wisely while indulging occasionally in wild spending sprees. You enjoy exploring the mysteries of life, and your strong desire to increase your knowledge and collect facts and statistics requires that you spend a fair amount of time alone.

Your executive abilities enable you to be the person in charge. Whether in business, on committees, or working for a cause, you are definitely at your best in any leadership position. You are inherently conservative and traditional, and your roots are important to you. You nurture close family ties and form friendships for a lifetime, and you will put forth great effort to see to it that your mate and children live the good life.

At your *best*, you are commanding, efficient, benevolent, discerning, competent, principled, self-confident, shrewd, persevering, persuasive, self-reliant, loyal, and quite beguiling!

At your *worst*, you *might* be impatient, vengeful, petty, excessively judgmental, repressive, controlling, uncaring, and/or ill-mannered.

IF YOU WERE BORN ON THE 18TH OF ANY MONTH

You are a multi-talented powerhouse of wisdom, strength, and courage! Observant and analytical, your perceptions of others are quite accurate, and your natural business acumen is equally impressive.

You are capable of far-reaching compassion and understanding for your fellow humans, and you are especially moved by those you deem to be helpless or suffering. Calm and self-possessed most of the time, it takes a lot to bring out your Mt. Vesuvius temper, but those who know you well have seen this side of you. A skilled orator, words are your greatest asset as well as your greatest weapon, and you definitely can enjoy an occasional argument or challenging debate. In fact, your strong code of ethics and principled nature can readily set you at odds with others. You dislike advice of any kind, preferring to be your own counsel. Whatever you decide to pursue, you can succeed at just about anything, if you make up your mind to do it.

Whether you are a stay-at-home housewife or an on-the-go world traveler, you are a prominent and commanding force in your environment. Travel and change are a must for your personal solace and, although the routine and predictability of the domestic side of life hold little interest for you, you are a devoted and loving mate and parent.

At your *best*, you are loving, compassionate, broad-minded, devoted, cooperative, sympathetic, self-sacrificing, philanthropic, humble, and wholly captivating!

At your *worst*, you *might* be cynical, overly critical of others, insincere, conceited, possessive, oppressive, and exhibit erratic emotional displays.

IF YOU WERE BORN ON THE 19TH OF ANY MONTH

Your adventuresome spirit and individualism make you yearn for variety and change. If you are not altering your personal environment in some way, you find other ways to experience change, such as traveling or expanding your knowledge. No matter how many setbacks you may experience in your lifetime, your regenerative powers, coupled with your strong will, perseverance, and tenacity, allow you to meet any challenge and eventually succeed at your endeavors. In fact, your verbal persuasiveness and awareness of human nature enable you to skillfully manipulate others to your way of thinking.

You possess a strong sense of responsibility when you are committed to something, but you do not like convention and cannot abide being confined in the same environment for long. Although you are logical, intelligent, and witty, your emotional temperament can zigzag from intense love to scathing dislike in one afternoon. Adamantly independent, you cannot, and will not, succumb to a subservient or passive role.

Strong and abiding friendships for you are very few, but you have many casual relationships that afford you the flexibility you crave to be there or not, at your preference. You have an invincible bond with your family and mate; and from that love, you learn to be more selfless, compassionate, and understanding.

At your *best*, you are wonderfully imaginative, determined, innovative, original, pioneering, noble, courageous, self-reliant, individualistic, progressive, an achiever, charming, and totally irresistible!

At your *worst*, you *might* be very stubborn, selfish, a know-it-all, jealous, indifferent, vain, pretentious, and/or greedy.

IF YOU WERE BORN ON THE 20TH OF ANY MONTH

Your warm-hearted, gentle, and congenial nature is attractive to both sexes, and you will collect and retain many friends in your lifetime. Behind your laid-back, unassuming demeanor lies a radar-like awareness and high-tuned instinctiveness. In fact, you can be like a human computer/barometer, collecting vast amounts of data from your surroundings while, at the same time, instantaneously sensing the moods and attitudes of everyone in your environment.

Sometimes you can be cantankerous and a bit stubborn, but mostly you like to promote harmony and camaraderie, and you are always able to understand both sides in a conflict. Your sensitive emotional constitution requires retreats to the country or other quiet places to rejuvenate.

An exceptional ability in the culinary arts is fostered by your strong need to nurture and give to others. Companionship, friendships, and family relations are the most important aspects of your life, and you are a devoted, loving, sometimes self-sacrificing, mate and parent.

At your *best*, you are a peacemaker, generous, tactful, considerate, modest, gracious, outgoing, scrupulous, nurturing, hospitable, agreeable, adaptable, and completely delightful!

At your *worst*, you *might* be excessively vacillating, a busybody, overly sensitive, fault-finding, apathetic, and unemotional.

IF YOU WERE BORN ON THE 21ST OF ANY MONTH

You enjoy entertaining and being entertained. An active social life is a must for you, and your pleasing, charming personality fits in anywhere. As a host or hostess, you are exceptional, instinctively knowing how to see to it that everyone has a good time and feels comfortable. Your extraordinary imagination, captivating storytelling abilities, and dramatic delivery guarantee that you will be the center of attention much of the time.

Optimistic, courageous, and a bit of a dreamer, you are attracted to ideas and schemes that are exciting, challenging, and even risky. Because you are so multitalented, you must guard against scattering your energies by trying to do too many things at once. Your strong artistic and musical inclinations attract you to beauty and the performing arts. You also love traveling and exploring the earth and its many and varied cultures.

You tend to be choosy about your close friends and your mate, and, although you have a flirtatious side, you are faithful when in love. As a parent, you can be strict but your fun-loving, sometimes childlike, nature is a major plus as it enables you to enjoy children's favorite pastimes and games almost as much as they do.

At your *best*, you are optimistic, witty, inspiring, sociable, self-expressive, creative, articulate, fun-loving, stylish, hospitable, sympathetic, amusing, and provocatively charming!

At your *worst*, you *might* be very extravagant, selfish, scattered, arrogant, a gossip, insincere, and/or excessively vain.

IF YOU WERE BORN ON THE 22ND OF ANY MONTH

You can exhibit extraordinary discipline, energy, logic, and sensitivity. For your psychological well-being, it is essential for you to follow a plan or daily routine, and you need orderly, functional surroundings. Although your political and philosophical leanings are usually conservative and conventional, your uncanny intuition can inspire insights and perceptions that are sometimes beyond the norm.

Your tendency to idealize is complemented by unwavering self-confidence and tenacity that enable you to accomplish the far-reaching goals you set for yourself. You will work harder and longer than almost anyone else but can become emotionally unraveled if you don't get enough rest. In order to realign your mental and emotional equilibrium, you may need to take time to be alone on occasion.

If anyone offends your sense of justice or basic moral beliefs, you can be a most formidable adversary. Your most endearing qualities are your wit, easygoing disposition, and your ability to make others laugh, sometimes through mimicry.

Home and family relations give you a sense of worthiness and security, and you are a supportive and loving parent and mate.

At your *best* you are prudent, organized, ethical, determined, honest, compliant, dutiful, orderly, patient, very successful, and passion-evoking!

At your *worst*, you *might* be insecure, provincial, opinionated, turbulent, self-important, exaggerating, and/or fanatical.

IF YOU WERE BORN ON THE 23RD OF ANY MONTH

You possess a nurturing, fun-loving, freedom-oriented spirit. The turbocharged energy force within makes it difficult for you to sit quietly. Your intelligent, quick mind constantly churns out original ideas and plans, and you possess awesome problem-solving skills. You enjoy learning and gathering information in all areas of life, but your impatient nature may result in your collecting only superficial information and knowledge.

Multitalented and self-sufficient, you find many ways to make a living and usually enjoy a relatively independent existence. Being a communicator, you enjoy expressing your opinions, but you do not like to argue. Therefore, you can readily adapt to different or difficult opposing concepts without becoming angry. You always make the best of every situation and are an especially good-natured companion.

You enjoy family relations but do not allow yourself to be bound by conventional or customary constraints. Your people-oriented personality enjoys entertaining and, although you accumulate many friends, your confidants are few—you like to keep your personal life very private. You are a caring, nurturing parent and derive some of your greatest pleasure from raising children.

At your *best*, you are progressive, resourceful, energetic, discerning, quick-witted, adaptable, gracious, charismatic, adventurous, hospitable, skillful, and delightfully irresistible!

At your *worst*, you *might* be unpredictable, overindulgent, high-strung, thoughtless, and thrill-seeking.

IF YOU WERE BORN ON THE 24TH OF ANY MONTH

You are charming, social, witty, and much more of a lover than a fighter. Your love of luxury and beautiful things gives you an affinity for museums and art galleries, gourmet restaurants, and everything else that appeals to the senses. You are constantly on the go but dislike accounting for your time or punching a time clock.

You take life seriously and sometimes assume too many responsibilities. This can cause you to develop an overprotective, self-righteous nature that makes you believe you have the right solutions for everything. Sound, unwavering principles and values support your beliefs in honor, order, hard work, and commitment. If your sense of fairness and justice are offended, you can become stubborn and argumentative. You will, however, lend a sympathetic ear to anyone and, when asked, offer practical and compassionate advice. A penchant to be a bit dramatic tends to make you magnify your joys and sorrows.

Upholding family and social traditions is important to you. Your home, family, and friends are the stabilizing forces in your life, and you will do more than your share to ensure that they are well cared for and secure. You are patient with children and a natural teacher, therefore making you a very good parent.

At your *best*, you are conciliatory, unselfish, charming, truthful, compassionate, artistic, a humanitarian, responsible, dutiful, ethical, considerate, loyal, charitable, sentimental, and irresistibly appealing!

At your *worst*, you *might* be overly dependent, a bit of a martyr, emotionally smothering, offensively self-righteous, and a worrier.

IF YOU WERE BORN ON THE 25TH OF ANY MONTH

You are witty and wise, and you wonder about everything! Your natural lust for knowledge is equal only to your reservoir of innate wisdom. You are highly intuitive, have an uncanny ability to perceive the moods and thoughts of others, and see through false pretensions.

Your unique personality fits in anywhere, and you are an interesting conversationalist. However, you also have an aloof, quiet side that requires time alone to sort out and analyze the myriad of thoughts and ideas in your mind. You tend to repress your feelings and emotions and need an artistic, scientific, or sports outlet to bring a balance to your psyche. You like spending time in the country and will find your greatest inner peace when close to nature or the sea.

You are trustworthy, loyal, honest, and prone to being a perfectionist. If you are not careful, your philosophical, moral, and spiritual high standards can make it difficult for you to accept and tolerate others' views and lifestyles. Although you are not very physically and emotionally demonstrative, you are a devoted, responsible, and caring mate, parent, and friend.

At your *best*, you are dependable, broad-minded, creative, logical, learned, resourceful, a truth seeker, scholarly, perceptive, patient, gifted, a visionary, wise, clairvoyant, intriguing, interesting, and exciting!

At your *worst*, you *might* be superficial, noncommittal, a worrier, melancholy, aloof, and sarcastic.

IF YOU WERE BORN ON THE 26TH OF ANY MONTH

Your personality is like that of a five-star general—steadfast and in command, fond of protocol, and constantly organizing your troops to effect the grand plans and ideas your mind maps out. Highly intelligent, with strong leadership abilities, you will never be content in a subordinate position and usually find the ways and means to call your own shots.

You can attract money, power, and fame, especially if your focus is toward helping others in some way. Your greatest challenges are being overly judgmental and power-hungry. You are prone toward pomp and circumstance, and you will spend lavishly for a favorite cause or an intimate affair; but you can also go to extremes with frugality. Your desire for quality is complemented by your skill as a shopper, and your clothes and home usually showcase your talent and good taste.

Your strong humanitarian tendencies make you ever-ready to lend a helping hand to those in need. However, you are inclined to be very discerning about the company you keep, and your high-tuned intuition enables you to quickly ferret out those who walk to your quality drumbeat. You are a protective and caring, albeit regimental, parent and mate.

At your *best*, you are charitable, considerate, courageous, understanding, reliable, helpful, commanding, efficient, ethical, a pacifist, straightforward, highly successful, and extraordinarily captivating!

At your *worst*, you *might* be judgmental, overbearing, avaricious, vindictive, jealous, and power-hungry.

IF YOU WERE BORN ON THE 27TH OF ANY MONTH

Like Old King Cole, you are a merry old soul, and you possess vast innate knowledge and extraordinary perceptivity. Because of these natural gifts, you can develop a sense of superiority toward others, but this tendency is usually tempered by a highly compassionate and generous nature. Your capabilities and interests are varied, and you can do anything well if you set your mind to it. Your biggest challenge is deciding on which of your many talents to focus. Travel and change are essential to your sense of well-being.

Your quick intellect and genteel charm enable you to impress and influence others, and you mix easily with everyone. However, you tend to be ultraconservative or ultraliberal and must guard against becoming self-righteous and intolerant of others' views and lifestyles.

Your quiet strength, diplomacy, and affectionate nature make you a good marriage partner, but you frequently need time alone to do your own thing. It is likely that you have a cultural or sports hobby that consumes much of your spare time. You are comfortable adhering to the conventions of society and tend to be conservative and somewhat provincial with regard to your family and home life.

At your *best*, you are adventurous, enthusiastic, inspiring, creative, generous, understanding, noble, humble, a romantic, and very sensual!

At your *worst*, you *might* be moody, self-pitying, selfish, stubborn, hot-tempered, uncaring, and/or egotistical.

IF YOU WERE BORN ON THE 28TH OF ANY MONTH

You are charming, a born diplomat, and your character is that of an achiever and a leader. You attract a host of friends, from the most unconventional to the most conforming, and, like your friends, you express an array of personality qualities: You are courageous and bold, yet shy and reserved; you are conservative but also a risk taker, and you love personal recognition, yet demand a high-degree of privacy.

Although your principles of life are sound, your strong-willed, freedom-oriented nature enables you to break with tradition in order to accomplish your goals and avoid the constraints of a 9-5 job. You are a dreamer who can make your wildest dreams come true.

You have high ideals and definite, strong opinions, but your compassionate, affectionate nature makes you a soft touch, always willing to help, especially friends and family members. Your home and family relations are a high priority to you, and you treat them with the utmost consideration. As a parent, you are nurturing, loving, and a disciplinarian.

At your *best*, you are inventive, individualistic, determined, organized, foresighted, a self-starter, a leader, bold, courageous, progressive, high-minded, exciting, and gorgeous!

At your *worst*, you *might* be demanding, arrogant, self-indulgent, militant, possessive, jealous, and/or controlling.

IF YOU WERE BORN ON THE 29TH OF ANY MONTH

Your gentle, sensitive nature is complemented by a combination of energy and charisma that draws people to you like a magnet. You enjoy learning and can inspire others with your reservoir of knowledge and insight. You are a capable leader, and with your unbridled enthusiasm and verbal eloquence, can easily motivate others to help with a cause you hold dear or support an opinion you espouse.

You are frequently called upon to be the "big shoulders" for others, listening to their problems, and you possess a sixth sense that helps you offer wise and useful advice. Your moods may be somewhat unpredictable, including a quick but short-lived temper, but you are a peace lover at heart and will do your best to maintain a harmonious atmosphere.

Home is where your heart lies, and stability in all your relationships is essential to your psychological well-being. As a mate and parent, you are nurturing, considerate, and understanding, and your desire to give and receive love is profound and enduring.

At your *best*, you are verbally persuasive, highly spiritual, outgoing, idealistic, imaginative, poetic, cooperative, gracious, modest, progressive, alluring, and beguiling!

At your *worst*, you *might* be fanatical, insensitive, condescending, very high strung, and/or a con artist.

IF YOU WERE BORN ON THE 30TH OF ANY MONTH

You are intelligent, creative, fun-loving, and blessed with a great sense of humor. Expressing yourself is essential to your happiness, and sometimes you do this with a dramatic flair. You enjoy social gatherings and, because of your extraordinary exuberance and vitality, you usually stand out in a crowd and tend to make a lasting impression on those who meet you.

Unless you are involved in a career that you enjoy—like working in the world of communication or doing something creative—you are inclined to expend as little effort as necessary to get the job done. Manual labor is definitely not your calling. You are usually fastidious and disciplined about your environment, attire, and physical self, or you are just the opposite—

filling your days with too many things to pay attention to the small details, like making your bed or tidying your office.

You enjoy physical activities and are usually involved in an exercise or athletic program. You are a wonderful companion, and your friends are numerous. Although your charm and charisma draw more than your share of admirers, you are fundamentally a faithful love mate and marriage partner. You have a natural affinity with children and are an inspiring, conscientious, and fun-filled parent, albeit a strong disciplinarian.

At your *best*, you are happy-go-lucky, friendly, artistic, fashionable, witty, charming, articulate, optimistic, inspirational, gracious, congenial, romantic, affectionate, and very foxy!

At your *worst*, you *might* be extravagant, insincere, self-centered, vain, garrulous, picky, highly critical of others, overly fastidious, and a supreme disciplinarian.

IF YOU WERE BORN ON THE 31ST OF ANY MONTH

You are creative, innovative, and possess a vast amount of knowledge. Dependable and reliable, you are a creature of habit, and you enjoy routine. In fact, adhering to a schedule actually gives you a sense of security. However, an independent nature and your nonconformist attitude can make you rather unpredictable and changeable at times, especially to those who think they have you figured out.

You enjoy traveling and learning about different cultures, but you also like the quiet comforts of your home life. Your capable, thorough, and precision-oriented abilities make you definite leadership material, and you usually gravitate into a managerial or executive position in your career. Honest, trustworthy, self-confident, and a dedicated worker, you have the personality to achieve major success in your professional life. The acquisition of money is important to you, as it represents the fruits of your efforts, and you are usually very careful about how you spend it.

You are private about your personal life and tend to be a loyal and dependable friend and mate. A stable home and supportive family are essential for your complete happiness.

At your *best*, you are competent, practical, devoted, efficient, industrious, methodical, organized, principled, scrupulous, and you can be a great lover!

At your *worst*, you *might* be excessively argumentative, provincial, unimaginative, didactic, stubborn, and unsociable.

Chapter 5

The Attitude Number

Your "Inside" Self's Personal Attitude
(The Month You Were Born Added to the Day of the Month You Were Born)

The Attitude number is most powerful in the first phase of your life, which lasts from birth up to the age of 36, depending on your Destiny number (see calculation below). It offers an understanding of how and why you act and react the way you do with family members, friends, and in social situations. It can also offer an understanding of why you are (were) a good student or why you are (were) unduly restless and disinterested throughout your school years. In some instances, this "attitude" can be carried forward into your 40s and 50s, but it usually begins to lose some of its strength once you have passed out of your first phase of life.

The Attitude number is found by adding the month you were born to the day you were born. If you were born in the months of October, November, or December, reduce the number of each month to a single digit, as follows:

October	=	10 and 1 + 0 = 1
November	=	11 and 1 + 1 = 2
December	=	12 and 1 + 2 = 3

Example: If you were born on August 13, your Attitude number would be calculated as follows: 8 (August) + 4 (1+3 = 4) = 12 and 1 + 2 = 3. Your Attitude number is 3. If you were born on November 25, add 2 (November) + 7 (2+5 = 7), which equals 9. Your Attitude number is 9. If a month and day of birth reduce to the Master numbers of 11 or 22, do not reduce those numbers to a single because they are Master number vibrations.

To determine when you pass out of your first phase of life and into your second phase of life, subtract your Destiny number from 36.

Examples: If your Destiny number is 4, you would pass into your second phase of life at the age of 32 (36 minus 4 = 32). If your Destiny number is 9, you would pass into your second phase at the age of 27 (36 minus 9 = 27).

My Attitude Number Is: _____

DEFINITIONS OF ATTITUDE NUMBERS 1 THROUGH 9, 11 AND 22 FOLLOW

ATTITUDE NUMBER 1

As a baby, you probably walked and talked early and wanted to take charge of your own life almost from the time you arrived! Those with a 1-Attitude are very precocious and clever, even as children. Although you possess a strong will and a sometimes stubborn nature, you also have a sensitive and sweet disposition. The good news is that you are exceptionally creative and inventive; and with a positive focus, you can accomplish *big* things during this powerful first phase of your life. The not-so-good news is that your strong need for independence can cause you to ignore advice and refuse help from those who want the best for you. You may even have to learn a lesson or two the hard way before you acknowledge that accepting the advice you are offered can actually make your life easier. Basically, this Attitude vibration gives you strong individuality, determination, stamina, and the energy to achieve *any* goal you set for yourself. So, be innovative, blaze a few trails, break records, and soar to heights that others only imagine . . . because YOU CAN DO IT!

ATTITUDE NUMBER 2

This is a "people-pleaser" Attitude number in the most positive sense. You are nurturing, caring, and kind. In fact, many of you are the peacemakers in your family. In your early years, you require less adult supervision than others because you usually try hard to do your best in any situation, and you never complain. You are also an especially good caretaker of small children, seniors, and animals. Your sensitive nature is like an emotional sponge that soaks up every nuance and vibe in your atmosphere. In fact, this high-tuned awareness may sometimes jumble your nervous system. Music of any kind, but especially classical music, helps to bring your out-of-sync spirit back into balance. Occasionally, you may be a little moody (because the 2 is ruled by the mood-provoking Moon) but overall, your Attitude should be more of a pleasure than a problem for those who know and love you. The best attribute of this Attitude vibration is your sensitivity. It gives you compassion, understanding, and the desire to bring comfort and solace to others, and that is truly admirable!

ATTITUDE NUMBER 3

You may have been very shy as a small child, but once you discovered the clever imagination you possess and how captivating you can be with words, communication in one way or another became a *must*! Your biggest challenge in life may be channeling your wonderful imagination in one direction only. You see, the 3 represents creative communication, and therefore drawing, painting, playing a musical instrument, singing, acting, and dancing are all natural talents for those with a 3-Attitude. And all things that glitter, sparkle, shine, fly, dance, gallop, hop, or run can arouse your curiosity and appeal to your sense of adventure. Because of your ever-present desire for fun and excitement, many of you are inclined to scatter your energies in too many directions. When you finally do set a goal, however, you can be extraordinarily disciplined and committed to seeing it through. Your sweet charm and exuberant spirit make you popular with everyone, and this happy-go-lucky vibration can be like a breath of fresh air to those you meet. Spread it around!

ATTITUDE NUMBER 4

Duty, responsibility, purpose, determination, self-motivation, and steadfast focus are the awesome qualities associated with this Attitude vibe. When you are inspired, you can accomplish *grand* things! But when you are *not*, no one can get you to budge! Although this is the most industrious vibration, it can also be the laziest if your interest has not been ignited. Another interesting dichotomy of the 4-Attitude is that you like to be organized, but you're not very inclined to be neat and orderly. As you mature, you slowly but surely learn that you can't have one without the other. Although you can be the consummate contrarian and are often inclined to offer your opinions in a blunt, straightforward fashion that can be unnerving to some, you also have a caring, loyal, and sympathetic side to your personality. Your quirky sense of humor and maverick-like nature are the elements of this Attitude number that prompt your sometimes shocking boldness. And, you can show great fortitude in the face of monumental opposition or challenge. You have what it takes to be *great*! Believe it!

ATTITUDE NUMBER 5

This highly charged and energized Attitude number creates an insatiable need for mental stimulation and physical activity. Your interest and curiosity are enormous, and you tend to be someone who is "in-the-know," on-the-go, and as up with the times as anyone! This "fast-lane force" can cause you to eat, drink, shop, work and, alas, drive too fast most of the time. Patience and self-control are the most essential qualities those with this "speedy Gonzales" tendency need to develop and nurture. Learning to focus on one task until it's completed is one way to help yourself acquire greater stability and patience. Broad-minded and adaptable, you tend to have many friends, and you especially enjoy companions who are of varying religious, ethnic, and cultural backgrounds. Your positive, forward-thinking disposition, natural charisma and adept verbal skills make you interesting, entertaining, and attractive to just about everyone. And when you are enthusiastic about *anything*, you can move the masses to help promote your cause. Make yourself one of your favorite causes!

ATTITUDE NUMBER 6

You have a humanitarian nature, and from a very early age, express a decided interest in caring for everything that seems to need your help. In fact, even as a child, you can be an especially competent and capable caretaker of children, the home, and animals. Being responsible and conscientious is second nature to you, and you usually enjoy doing things with your family and being useful—even, amazingly, during your teen years. Your gifted teaching skills and natural patience may draw you into volunteer work in schools, hospitals, and the like. Most with 6-Attitudes are very good students, and many of you become the "teacher's pet" because of your penchant to please others. Issues around fairness and justice are concerns that can cause you to become argumentative and even defiant, especially if you feel your personal values and ethical standards are being compromised. Friendship is very important to you; and with this Attitude, you are one of the best friends anyone could have! Sometimes you can take life a little too seriously for your own good. Try to take some time out now and then to do things that make you feel emotionally and physically nourished and happy. You deserve it!

ATTITUDE NUMBER 7

There are two types of expression under this vibration. One is an out-going, extra-cheery, and friendly person who sometimes may become known as the "class clown." The other is a quiet, serious, secretive, and sometimes slightly-nerdy individual. Whichever type you seem to be, one thing is for sure: You are not ordinary. The 7 rules genius, and therein lies the reason you may seem (and feel) different than others. Take the author's word for it—you are different, and that's okay! Even though you may feel left out or that you don't fit with the "in-crowd," understand that you have the potential to do something exceptional because of your unique way of learning and viewing things. In the earliest stage of your life, you may find it almost impossible to express your deepest feelings, and that Attitude can carry forward even into young adulthood. However, many with 7-Attitude love to learn and are very creative. Writing poetry, drawing, painting, and/or involving yourself in theatrical studies are all ways to help you express your interesting, unique, and insightful (sometimes even brilliant) ideas, thoughts, and feelings. Expanding your knowledge is the foremost prerequisite of this brainy Attitude vibration. Do whatever it takes to accomplish that, and you will *never* regret it!

ATTITUDE NUMBER 8

With an 8-Attitude, you can go two ways: (1) You may be a most dutiful, goody-two-shoes person in your early years (and well-liked, too), or (2) you may be a rebel without a cause. An 8- Attitude guarantees that whatever you give out will come back to you instantaneously; therefore, it is important that you become very aware of what signals you're sending out! The 8 is the number of the director or the "chairman of the board," so it is natural for you to give orders and take charge of things. It is also natural for you to desire to *be somebody*! You may dream about fame and fortune and, guess what—this Attitude can take you there because the number 8 also rules money, power and notoriety! The bad news is that you still have to work for what you achieve—sometimes harder than you would like. But the harder you try, the higher you will rise. That's what the power of the 8 will do for you. The number 8 bestows extra good fortune through action! You have the golden star of success hanging over your head with this Attitude number. Let its penetrating rays infuse you with the self-confidence and faith that you can achieve your grandest dreams, and *you will*!

ATTITUDE NUMBER 9

You may have amazed your parents and teachers in your early years by your exceptional awareness. This Attitude number assumes a more adult-like nature than that of most other children and young adults. The 9 is associated with aristocracy and, therefore, you may develop a taste for fine things at a very early age—from 24-carat gold to Ferraris. Feelings of stress can occasionally cause you to have major temper outbursts (the 9 is ruled by Mars, the passion planet) or to feel depressed (which is usually suppressed anger). But most of you tend to do what is expected of you without complaint in order to alleviate anxiety and undue pressure. Helping and caring for others is a common role in the life of someone with a 9-Attitude. This is a "people-pleasing" Attitude number, so it is usually easy for people to enjoy your presence and company. On the negative side, this people-pleasing tendency may make it difficult for you to be assertive or to stand up for your own ideals as you mature. However, it also sets the stage for you to learn how to handle yourself with the poise and confidence needed to become a respected and acknowledged individual. Since you appreciate the *best* that life has to offer, understand that *you* can be that, too!

ATTITUDE NUMBER 11

This Attitude number is comparable to the 2-Attitude. You are kind, considerate, and caring toward others, and you are very sensitive! In fact, this vibration wires you with two invisible, high-tuned antennas that allow you to "receive" virtually every feeling and sensation in your environment. You are like an atmospheric sponge, soaking up all the vibes—good or bad—in your surroundings. Because of this, you may sometimes feel hyperactive, overstimulated, and overly sensitive and, in actuality, you *are*! You can, however, realign your psyche by listening to music (especially classical) because it is like a soothing balm for your nervous system. It is natural for you to want peace and quiet in your environment and, therefore, it is important that you have a place where you can go to be alone to collect your thoughts and feelings. If and when you learn to meditate, it will open up your intuitive senses, and you will be able to comprehend all aspects of life with much greater insight and awareness. Once that occurs, you will instinctively know how to help those who come to you with personal problems. This capability is a gift, and you should strive to use it only in the most conscientious and humble fashion. It is the "angel" vibration.

ATTITUDE NUMBER 22

You can be the most dutiful and responsible kid on the block or the most stubborn and unmanageable—or both! Even if you don't outwardly express your need to make your own decisions or your innate dislike for rules, you will inwardly harbor those thoughts. In fact, you usually find a way to alter the rules ever so slightly to suit your own preferences. It's not that you are a born troublemaker, it's just that you emphatically know what you do and don't like. There is also a conscientious, diligent persona that lurks within your steadfast, sometimes arbitrary Attitude. Those who know you well love you for the complex person you can be. This Attitude number can take you to great heights at a very early age if you find a focus that holds your interest. You can be a champion athlete or a super whiz-kid entrepreneur! This vibration may also deliver some very harsh life lessons, primarily due to your tendency to go against rules and conventional wisdom. This is a very high spiritual vibration and sometimes requires you to learn lessons the hard way in order to awaken you to your better self and your own spiritual quest. More than any other number vibration, this one gives you the power to resoundingly elevate yourself or to cast your fate to the wind in a veil of unruly willfulness. Which path will *you* choose?

Chapter 6

Your Name: The "You" That People See

The Character

(The Number Derived from the Total Addition of All the Letters in Your Name)

The Soul Urge

(The Number Derived from Adding the Vowels in Your Name)

and

The Hidden Agenda

(The Number Derived from the Consonants in Your Name)

Use the following alphabet grid to determine your Character, Soul Urge, and Hidden Agenda numbers. To calculate the Character number, add together all the numbers associated with the letters in the full name from birth and reduce that number to a single digit, or a Master number, where appropriate. (Refer to Chapter 2 for a detailed example of this calculation.)

1	2	3	4	5	6	7	8	9
A	B	C	D	E	F	G	H	I
J	K	L	M	N	O	P	Q	R
S	T	U	V	W	X	Y	Z	

Once you have determined your Character number, enter it below for future reference:

THE CHARACTER

(THE MOST PROMINENT QUALITIES AND CHARACTER YOU EXHIBIT IN THE OUTSIDE WORLD)

The Character number is the strongest vibration you exhibit in your out-side world, i.e.; socially and on-the-job. It is the persona you present in public, along with the Soul Urge and Hidden Agenda vibrations, that projects how you will impress those who know you less intimately than family and friends. Hopefully, most of you will not exhibit the negative-expression personality associated with your number, but it is helpful to be aware of the most negative aspects of each number that are expressed in their lower form.

Example: First, let's determine the Character number, which is found by adding together all numbers associated with the letters in your given name (specifically, the name that is on your birth certificate). The above diagram is used to find the number equivalent for each letter in your name.

Using the name **Samantha Kay Johnson** as an example, it works like this:

1	1	4	1	5	2	8	1		2	1	7		1	6	8	5	1	6	5
S	A	M	A	N	T	H	A		K	A	Y		J	O	H	N	S	O	N

First, add all the numbers together in the first name:

1 + 1 + 4 + 1 + 5 + 2 + 8 + 1 = 23
S   A   M   A   N   T   H   A

Then, add all the numbers together in the middle name:

2 + 1 + 7 = 10
K   A   Y

Then, add all the numbers together in the last name:

1 + 6 + 8 + 5 + 1 + 6 + 5 = 32
J   O   H   N   S   O   N

Next, add the compound numbers of each name together:

Samantha	=	23
Kay	=	10

Johnson	=	32
Total	=	65

Now, reduce that number to a single digit:

6 + 5 = 11

Samantha's Character number is 11. In this case, the number is not reduced to a single digit because it is a Master number, which is referred to above.

My Character Number Is: _____

DESCRIPTIONS OF THE CHARACTER NUMBERS FOLLOW

CHARACTER NUMBER 1

MOST POSITIVE EXPRESSION: An original, creative leader.

Independent, self-confident, ambitious and strong-willed, you possess pronounced leadership abilities! You are better than most (or the best) at whatever you do because you like the personal latitude that you are afforded in elevated positions. As a natural promoter, you especially like to champion your own ingenious ideas, concepts, and products, and many of you become successful entrepreneurs. Being self-employed is a natural for anyone with a 1-Character number and, once you have set your focus on a career endeavor, you will pursue it with gusto! Many of you enjoy gathering facts on topics that interest you. Having an array of information at your disposal gives you the ability to be a captivating and original teacher and/or lecturer.

Negatively expressed, this influence can make you domineering, overly aggressive, and excessively competitive. Stubborn and lazy are other aspects that you might exhibit when you do not like or want to carry out the responsibilities or job you are assigned.

AFFIRMATION: When I feel independent and am in control of my life, I am far less likely to be stubborn or lazy or try to control others!

CHARACTER NUMBER 2

MOST POSITIVE EXPRESSION: A naturally diplomatic, good-natured ambassador for the people.

You are a natural peacemaker, and your outward expression is kind, considerate, patient, and congenial. You can be an effective counselor or teacher, and your conscientious, cooperative nature is well-suited to working with the public or for assuming administrative and managerial positions. Your pleasant and accommodating manner makes it easy for you to adapt to people and situations, and you can be an especially congenial and cooperative co-worker, friend, companion, and mate. An affinity for details and organization gives you exceptional qualifications to be administrators or group facilitators. You are the proverbial team player—always compliant, careful, and considerate of others' feelings and needs.

Negatively expressed, when your sensitive nature takes over, you may demand constant attention and approval of others. Some of you may find it difficult to stand up for yourself and may let others take advantage of your good nature, over and over again.

AFFIRMATION: I take pleasure in being a giver and a peacemaker, but I am not a pushover!

CHARACTER NUMBER 3

MOST POSITIVE EXPRESSION: An optimistic, enthusiastic, and creative communicator.

You are a skilled communicator who is charming, energetic, optimistic, and imaginative. You love the spotlight, and the majority of you are natural entertainers. One thing is certain, you *must* communicate in one form or another. Acting, writing, singing, painting, or becoming a computer whiz are excellent outlets for your exceptionally creative and imaginative mental and verbal faculties. Your gregarious, happy-go-lucky attitude is inspiring and uplifting to others, and many of you find great success in occupations that have a high degree of public contact. Sales, marketing, and advertising are other areas of endeavor that can benefit from your natural gifts.

Negatively expressed, you can be excessively talkative and seemingly incapable of listening to what others have to say, childish, and inordinately vain and superficial. Being trivial and overly critical of others are other unattractive features of this Character number.

AFFIRMATION: I will practice encouraging others rather than being critical and will try to be attentive rather than attention-seeking!

CHARACTER NUMBER 4

MOST POSITIVE EXPRESSION: A conscientious, organized, reliable worker and dedicated friend.

You can be *the most* dependable, honest, hard-working individual around. Your logical, systematic mind and pronounced abilities for developing and maintaining order help you to pursue your goals and commitments with steadfast determination and perseverance to the finish! Punctuality, practicality, and patience with details are other qualities that make you a superlative employee, employer, co-worker, and friend. Collecting and retaining facts on a broad array of topics enables you to be an especially interesting conversationalist, when you *want* to be. Once you open up and join in social fun, your wry sense of humor and engaging wit are traits that make you very appealing.

Negatively expressed, you can be ultrastubborn, bossy, contrary, narrow-minded, show interest only in work-related matters, and a social "zero." Some of you get so caught up in your own mire of dissatisfaction and discontent that you feel most comfortable avoiding the social scene altogether.

AFFIRMATION: Everyone benefits (family, friends, and me) when I spend a certain amount of time each day in a pleasurable pastime and/or socializing!

CHARACTER NUMBER 5

MOST POSITIVE EXPRESSION: A socially charming, adaptable and stylish trendsetter.

Your outgoing, energetic, and enthusiastic personality, coupled with your clever intellect, make you engaging, interesting, and entertaining to almost everyone. A driving need to keep abreast of the times and trends enables you to easily impress others by imparting snippets of news and other information that make it appear as if you know something about virtually everything. Sales, public speaking, and entertaining are career endeavors that give you the greatest ability to use your knowledge and verbal prowess to captivate and win others to your way of thinking. Versatility and adaptability are other attributes that help you gain a much-desired social and community acceptance.

Negatively expressed, you may have a strong propensity to exaggerating the truth. You can also be excessively critical and/or sarcastic when you feel your clever repartee was not as appreciated by your audience as you would have liked it to be.

AFFIRMATION: I will avoid being critical and haughty by using my wonderful verbal abilities, charm, and quick wit to help, serve, and entertain others!

CHARACTER NUMBER 6

MOST POSITIVE EXPRESSION: A humanitarian, community-oriented, outstanding parent/teacher/human being.

Your congenial, caring, and hospitable nature makes you a very likeable individual indeed! Everyone you meet, including casual acquaintances, are the happy recipients of your generous, understanding, and comforting manner. Any occupation that involves working with the public, children, animals, or Mother Nature in general gives you an avenue to pursue your desire to help and be of service. A true humanitarian, you possess strong principles and a penchant for fairness and justice for all. Although your philosophy may be a bit idealistic and romantic, you have the ability to manifest your dreams through steadfast perseverance and persistent belief in your ideals. Your artistic proclivities enable you to see beauty in people and things where others cannot, and you have a decided talent for interior and exterior design.

Negatively expressed, you can be argumentative, self-righteous, and lack the desire to be nurturing in any way. You may lack the objectivity to understand that it is the "*shoulds*" (you *should* appreciate me more; you *should* be home more; you *should* think like I think because my way is right, etc.) that you impose on others that create the most disharmony and dissension in your environment.

AFFIRMATION: I will practice expressing unconditional love and acceptance of everyone, especially my family and friends, and understand that I will always receive back what I am giving out!

CHARACTER NUMBER 7

MOST POSITIVE EXPRESSION: A philosophically avant-garde, knowledge-seeking genius.

You may seem aloof and even haughty to those who don't know you, but that's just because you prefer to appear extremely dignified in your outward approach. You are very observant of others and, once you are comfortable at social events or on the job, you have plenty to say. Being the center of attention is not something you seek; and in social surroundings, you are most intrigued by and enjoy people who are either mysterious in some way or intellectually superior. Your astute, analytical, and knowledge-thirsty nature gives you the ability to be masterful in any endeavor you choose. Most of you are perfectionists who hone your craft or career to its highest level. The 7 is known as the symbol of genius, and those of you who have tapped into your full potential can have resounding success, especially in the fields of art and science.

Negatively expressed, you can be non-communicative, rebellious, reclusive, overly-critical, pessimistic, sarcastic, moody, and fearful. As if that weren't enough, when you gravitate to the low side of this number, you may also alienate others by becoming strange and eccentric.

AFFIRMATION: I will strive to be masterful in all my work endeavors and to be more open and welcoming to others!

CHARACTER NUMBER 8

MOST POSITIVE EXPRESSION: A commanding, classy, exemplary executive, judge, teacher-of-teachers.

The optimism and enthusiasm you can exude when enamored by an idea or a cause are unprecedented! You have a sixth sense that makes you a keen judge of people and enables you to analyze circumstances and situations with uncanny accuracy, sometimes before events happen. You are the teacher of teachers because of your precision-tough memory faculties and exemplary demeanor. You also possess what is called "the buyer's eye" because you can ferret out quality from among junk. Being efficient and organized, you naturally wend your way to a top spot in your established career endeavor, and your refined taste and penchant for quality can be seen in everything you do and own. Many of you champion the underdog and like to become involved in upstanding community causes and, although you believe in rules and regulations, you will also help to effect changes that benefit the masses.

Negatively expressed, you can be scheming and calculating for self-gain, petty in your judgments, and power-hungry. Other negative traits include a tendency to be oppressive, domineering, and controlling.

AFFIRMATION: I will use my exemplary taste and talents to improve my community. I will practice being more adaptable and accepting of people and things that don't share my strong values and code of ethics!

CHARACTER NUMBER 9

MOST POSITIVE EXPRESSION: A sage, aristocratic, socially pleasing humanitarian.

No one can be more pleasant and personally appealing than you! Because it is very important to you that people accept, appreciate, and RESPECT you, you do your best to show the impeccable manners and polished behavior of an aristocrat when you are in the public. Your naturally charming and sophisticated ways inspire others to look to you to be the representative of their causes and committees. The 9 vibration is very prevalent in the numerology charts of politicians, humanitarians, and community leaders. You are the proverbial "old soul" and possess vast innate wisdom and a heightened perceptivity that sets you apart from others.

Negatively expressed, you can be hot-tempered, arrogant, standoffish, and egotistical. You also dislike anyone telling you what or how to do *anything*, and you can use your verbally skilled, but sometimes lethal tongue, to provoke, insult, and psychologically injure those who oppose you or your opinions.

AFFIRMATION: I will greatly improve my self-appreciation by expressing myself in positive ways rather than with my temper or an anger-motivated tongue!

CHARACTER NUMBER 11

MOST POSITIVE EXPRESSION: An empathetic, understanding counselor or community leader.

This Master number gives you a natural high-minded, compassionate nature. Your innate ability to deliver sound and sage advice makes your character well-suited to counseling or being involved in a spiritual endeavor such as the ministry. The 11 is known as the number of "illumination" which means your name can be known and you may find yourself in the spotlight at different times in your lifetime. Your excellent command of language and inspirational use of words gives you the ability to motivate others to take positive actions for their own betterment. Your sensitivity and intuition are assets in work endeavors that require managing, teaching, lecturing, and working directly with the public.

Negatively expressed, you may use your high-tuned intuition to "psyche people out" or as a tool to con them to fulfill your own materialistic needs. Some of you can be very unrealistic, overly emotional, fearful, self-effacing, and reticent to accept change—even beneficial changes.

AFFIRMATION: I will be more open to my intuitive powers and more accepting of using my inner-voice for guidance!

CHARACTER NUMBER 22

MOST POSITIVE EXPRESSION: A high-minded builder of empires and spiritually-oriented organizer.

This is the symbol of the Master Builder. You are infused with tremendous power, energy, and a unique, unconventional way of viewing the world and solving problems. This Character number gives you an unprecedented ability to accomplish your dreams and goals by utilizing your innate gifts of logic, foresight, heightened perceptively, and the desire to work for the good of others. It's your unorthodox approach to life and work that enable you to become an unparalleled master in your career endeavor—you'll get things done no matter what. You definitely walk to the beat of your own drum, and you tend to mentally operate in a mode that is not always available to the average person. You have the mind of a great mathematician, statistician, physicist, or rocket scientist. Are you using all this wonderful God-given potential?

Negatively expressed, you may be very high-strung and nervous and have difficulty maintaining focus. You can have a tendency to live too much in the moment and, therefore, fail to learn from lessons of the past or look far enough ahead to avoid obvious problems. This powerful vibration can also be used to dominate, oppress, and con others.

AFFIRMATION: I will always try to be helpful to mankind and nature by utilizing my masterful faculties!

THE SOUL URGE

(THE SOULFUL DESIRE OF THE OUTSIDE SELF)

The Soul Urge is the second most powerful name number. It is determined by adding together (and reducing to a single digit, or a Master number) the VOWELS in your full name from birth. Its influence tenders a view of your instinctive, soulful self, and it reflects your values and priorities. It's the Character number's star point of motivation and inspiration.

Example: Once again, I have used **Samantha Kay Johnson** as our example:

```
  1   1         1   1 7   6           6
S A M A N T H A K A Y J O H N S O N
```

$1 + 1 + 1 + 1 + 7 + 6 + 6 = 23 = 2+3 = 5$

The Soul Urge number for Samantha Kay Johnson is 5.

My Soul Urge Number Is: _____

DESCRIPTIONS OF THE SOUL URGE NUMBERS FOLLOW

SOUL URGE NUMBER 1

Innovation, creativity, and leadership are the primary attributes of this Soul Urge number. It also bestows you with the self-confidence and courage to hazard a chance, to take risks, and to blaze trails! With this powerful vibration propelling you forward, you are determined to leave the competition behind! You thoroughly enjoy a challenge and, because of that, you tend to resist rules and restrictions, and/or the cautionary suggestions of others. Your single-minded focus is to *win* or *be somebody*, and there's no limit to what you can accomplish under this power-filled vibration!

SOUL URGE NUMBER 2

This is the vibration of peace, harmony, diplomacy, and bringing comfort to others. It activates within you a desire to cooperate, compromise, and be a team player. Because you tend to look at all sides of a situation, you attract people who need an understanding, compassionate shoulder to lean on. Listening to others' problems, exhibiting genuine concern, and giving kindhearted, understanding advice are the primary missions of this Soul Urge.

SOUL URGE NUMBER 3

The combination of abounding energy and an infectious enthusiasm for life are the components of this Soul Urge vibration that give you a sparkling and engaging personality. A bountifully creative imagination and passionate need to express yourself are other prevalent attributes associated with this influence. It also enhances your ability to work congenially and persuasively with others, and to concoct brilliant ideas and schemes! Those with a 3 Soul Urge also love to entertain, and you enjoy lively, busy social lives.

SOUL URGE NUMBER 4

The factors that make this Soul Urge special are honesty, dependability, and practicality. It's part of your nature to be devoted to your job and family, methodical and pragmatic. This vibration imbues you with steadfast determination, orderliness, and responsibility, and those attributes help you to achieve and master whatever you set out to accomplish. You weigh things carefully before moving ahead, but you are also willing to make necessary sacrifices to reach your goals. With this stabilizing force, you can effect a strong foundation for all of your ideas, plans, and desires.

SOUL URGE NUMBER 5

This Soul Urge guarantees that you will have an excitable and exciting spirit, abounding energy, and a progressive, broad-minded outlook on life. This is the vibration of resourcefulness and versatility, and you love to come up with new and unique approaches to old themes and/or the status quo. This restless, impatient, and spontaneous influence gives you a desire for effecting swift and dramatic changes in any area of life that needs an overhaul. You value independence and adventure, and you're always ready to experience life to the fullest.

SOUL URGE NUMBER 6

Being of service and feeling that you are doing something useful are the primary impulses of this Soul Urge vibration. Your responsible, generous, and sympathetic nature may lead you to teach, counsel, or perform holistic procedures that bring comfort and ease to others, and you are a thoughtful, caring friend. The 6 is associated with humanitarianism and, therefore, gives you a strong sense of kinship to the earth and all of mankind. Its force helps you to manifest beauty and harmony, and you strive to inspire others to feel the same way.

SOUL URGE NUMBER 7

This Soul Urge vibration arouses in you a desire to analyze, question, and research all the mysteries of life. It is associated with psychic abilities, intuition, and innate wisdom. It fosters in you the need to spend time alone engaging in quiet contemplation and introspection. Abstract, mystic, and avant-garde ideas and concepts are part of your everyday thinking, and you possess an ongoing interest in expanding your knowledge. You don't like small talk, and those who don't know you may think you are unfriendly or haughty.

SOUL URGE NUMBER 8

Your nature is to be serious, consistent, and driven. Quality and class are the cornerstones of your Soul Urge vibration. As a symbol of leadership and executive abilities, the grand power and aplomb of this Soul Urge can be impressive. Bound by the aspiration to achieve the greatest efficiency, order and finesse, this vibration encourages a calculating mind and an in-charge manner. Unstoppable ambition and keen judgment are two other factors that help to generate the inherent star potential in this mighty force.

SOUL URGE NUMBER 9

Aristocracy and gentility are synonymous with the 9 and, therefore, those with this Soul Urge vibration are conventional, congenial, dignified, charitable, and respectful. The 9 is also the number of the universal humanitarian and, because of that influence, you may aspire to help the great masses in some way. You need to feel that you are being useful, and you always try to look for the good in others. Those with 9s in their chart have come into this world to help and serve others before themselves and as your Soul Urge vibration, some of your outstanding gifts include compassion, superior intuitive skills, and "old soul" wisdom.

SOUL URGE NUMBER 11

As a Soul Urge vibration, the number 11 radiates the qualities of peace, harmony, idealism, beauty, and perfectionism. Being the symbol of the counselor, confidant, and minister, it resonates to the highest spiritual vibration and bestows in you the ability to listen with understanding and compassion. As a consequence, it acts as a beacon of light that attracts people with problems into your life, and you deal with them with kindness and understanding. High-tuned intuition, superlative perceptivity, prolific innate wisdom, and a strong extra-dimensional connection are other endowments of this wonderfully spiritual vibration.

SOUL URGE NUMBER 22

This is the Master number Soul Urge of the Master Builder. It inspires in you the desire to accomplish *significant* things to help mankind. It epitomizes humanitarianism, high-mindedness, leadership, superlative intelligence and perceptivity, and a universal outlook and approach to life. You want to make a huge difference! Logic and practicality, along with a steady, determined mentality, give this vibration its exemplary ability to achieve, and at times exceed, your most ambitious goals with masterful delivery.

THE HIDDEN AGENDA
(THE "SECRET DESIRE" OF THE OUTSIDE SELF)

The Hidden Agenda number (sometimes called the Inner Self), is just what it implies—the secret desire of the Character number persona. Derived from adding the CONSONANTS in the name from birth, it is a concealed force of expression behind the Character number and the Soul Urge number. It is another part of your unique numerological makeup, and being aware of it can provide further insight into how your numbers influence your behavior.

Example: **Samantha Kay Johnson** is used again as our example:

1		4		5	2	8		2			1		8	5	1		5
S	A	M	A	N	T	H	A	K	A	Y	J	O	H	N	S	O	N

Using Samantha's name, add together the 1 + 4 + 5 + 2 + 8 in the name Samantha, which equals 20. The only consonant in Kay is the K which equals 2. Finally, add the 1 + 8 + 5 + 1 + 5 in Johnson, which equals 20. Then add 20 + 2 + 20, which equals 42, and add 4 + 2 = 6.

The Hidden Agenda number for Samantha is 6.

My Hidden Agenda Number Is: _____

DEFINITIONS OF THE HIDDEN AGENDA NUMBER FOLLOW

HIDDEN AGENDA NUMBER 1

This vibration, although closeted, incites in you the desire to be independent, to break out on your own and find a way to stand out—either personally or professionally. It also instills in you the ability to be a leader or to innovate and create something totally original and unique using your own knowledge and expertise. However you manifest this camouflaged vibration, its subtle effect helps you establish your individuality.

HIDDEN AGENDA NUMBER 2

The "secret desire" of this Hidden Agenda is the longing for peace and harmony. It encourages a non-aggressive, cooperative, and congenial nature that helps you to effect those desires. The number 2 vibration bestows in you a natural sense of rhythm, a good sense of humor, and a desire to comfort others. As a consequence, your hidden aspirations may include a desire to be a chef, a B&B inn owner, a professional dancer, a standup comedian, or some other type of entertainer.

HIDDEN AGENDA NUMBER 3

Sailing the high seas, flying around the world, being the entertainer of the year, composing and singing a Top Ten hit, or writing the great American novel, may be just a few of the secret desires brewing in your Hidden Agenda vibration. The 3 is the symbol of Peter Pan, and lurking inside you is a child who never wants to grow up. Having fun, experiencing pleasure, being adventurous, and having freedom of expression are this vibration's primary motivators. Go for it!

HIDDEN AGENDA NUMBER 4

An ability to handle details proficiently and to be an excellent problem-solver are two functions that spark this stalwart and resolute Hidden Agenda into action. Logic, organization, and perseverance are other qualities of the 4 that come into play when you are manifesting the successful life you desire. Frills and thrills do not figure into the dreams of those with this Hidden Agenda vibration, although a hobby like collecting interesting and unique things, fishing or playing bridge and the like, may be the exception.

HIDDEN AGENDA NUMBER 5

Freedom with a capital F is the dominant desire of this Hidden Agenda vibration—freedom of speech, action, and thought, and particularly the freedom to be spontaneous—to just pick up and go whenever the whim hits. To enjoy wealth and to travel the world are other strong motivators of this vibration, too, and a desire to live life in the fast lane spurs this Hidden Agenda into action. When its force is let loose, there is no telling where a fiver will end up!

HIDDEN AGENDA NUMBER 6

The number 6 is associated with humanitarianism and being responsible to home, family, and community. The "secret desire" of this number involves a kind, deeply-giving nature. Lending a hand where needed, being a philanthropist, volunteering for causes that help children, animals, and Mother Earth, are all hidden desires of the 6's Hidden Agenda. This righteous force helps to ensure fair play and justice in all the circumstances and causes you care about so deeply.

HIDDEN AGENDA NUMBER 7

A desire to vastly increase your knowledge is the driving force behind this Hidden Agenda vibration. An unquenchable interest in one or all of the arts, the sciences, the philosophies, or the religions may be the impetus that finds you enrolling in classes or voraciously researching a particular subject. The 7 is representative of genius, the virtuoso, and the maestro. It is part of your birthright to aspire toward perfectionism and masterful accomplishment! Just *do* it!

HIDDEN AGENDA NUMBER 8

This Hidden Agenda vibration hides your strong desire for power, acclaim, and making huge amounts of money. So, you ask, doesn't everyone want these things? Not like you. You have an eye for quality and possess the distinction of being a closet class act. A less subtle characteristic of this vibration is your consuming desire for everyone to follow the rules! The 8 is, in fact, the watchguard of protocol and regulations. Quick and savvy judgments are also a proclivity of this powerful hidden force.

HIDDEN AGENDA NUMBER 9

This is the Hidden Agenda vibration of the closet aristocrat (and perhaps not so well-hidden if there are one or more 9s in your chart). Under this vibration, your innate nobility and finesse respond best in a genteel and cultured environment. You secretly desire the finest of everything—entertainment, clothing, jewelry, car, house, and neighborhood. This vibration also affords you an innate reservoir of knowledge that helps you make the right choices that allow you to move up the ladder of success in your chosen endeavor.

HIDDEN AGENDA NUMBER 11

This is a Master number Hidden Agenda vibration and, as such, you may have an underlying desire to counsel, minister, or participate in the healing arts. This vibration affords you an easier and quicker connection with the powerful forces of the universe, and you can use this to help yourself and others. Other gifts of this spiritually-charged vibration are your highly tuned intuition, profound understanding of others' feelings and concerns, and the ability to use your own wisdom and knowledge to help and heal those around you.

HIDDEN AGENDA NUMBER 22

This Master number Hidden Agenda vibration shrouds a motivation to help and serve your fellow humans in some measurable way. You may dream of building a philanthropic empire, working as a missionary, or volunteering your time to causes that help the masses. The Master Builder power of the 22 is as present in this hidden vibration as it is in the 22 Character or Destiny numbers. It is a strong and moving force that cannot be denied. Let its power inspire you to do *great* things!

Chapter 7
Your Divine Purpose

The Purpose number (which is determined by adding your Character number to your Destiny number) provides insight into how to take your innate numerological aspects to a higher level—particularly during the later years of your life. Although the Purpose Number is an underlying influence all throughout your life, it becomes strongest after you pass the age of 45 and move into your 50s. Sometime during your 40s, the "old soul" within begins to peek its head out of the cocoon of your past and create a kind of metamorphosis or "mid-life crisis." This old soul or archetypal self is driven to express, in a meaningful way, all the qualities that are inherent in your spirit from the time you came onto the earth plane. As you enter the years between 45 and 75, the Purpose number can be the guiding force to help you effect your life's most creative and, in some cases, elevated purpose.

My Divine Purpose Number is: _____

DEFINITIONS OF EACH PURPOSE NUMBER FOLLOW

PURPOSE NUMBER 1
LONG-RANGE MISSION: To leave behind a legacy of something you pioneered—a concept, a product, a foundation.

This is the number of the initiator, the innovator, and the pioneer. You should feel the compelling need to pioneer a unique idea, concept, product, or business. Whatever action you take or idea you proffer, it is likely to be appreciated by future generations. This is a most demanding and exciting purpose. So clean out that mental storage unit of inventions and ideas you've always wanted to put into action, and give them their day in the sun. Who knows, you may invent a better mousetrap or write the great American novel!

PURPOSE NUMBER 2

LONG-RANGE MISSION: To bring comfort and harmony to your fellow humans.

Your soulful purpose is to be a peacemaker. This influence promotes a desire to bring harmony and loving feelings to others. Your congenial style and team-player attitude can help set an example for others that will assist in settling disputes and bringing serenity and order to chaotic situations. Possessing exemplary skills as an arbitrator, mediator, or diplomat, you may eventually be recognized by your peers as someone who can successfully gain cooperative interaction and participation from others for causes in your community.

PURPOSE NUMBER 3

LONG-RANGE MISSION: To use your creative and imaginative talents to produce a product, an idea, a book, a film, or some other form of artful expression.

Part of your soulful purpose is to utilize your communication and artistic skills in ways that will help others to better appreciate their own creativity. Presenting more effective methods of communication is another motivation of this Purpose number. This strong creative influence may manifest itself on the stage in the form of entertainment or lectures, in publishing and/or video/movie production, in the fields of painting or sculpting, in various areas of fashion design, or even in the arena of handmade crafts.

PURPOSE NUMBER 4

LONG-RANGE MISSION: To build a stable foundation that helps people and has a humanitarian focus.

The number 4 is associated with solidification and stability. This influence inspires you to lay a strong foundation or pursue a way of life that will make a lasting contribution to society. The focus of this mission, whether as a result of a business or a type of teaching, a product or a concept, should be to contribute something worthwhile to the world through an organized and methodical approach.

PURPOSE NUMBER 5

LONG-RANGE MISSION: To help to effect progressive changes that make life better for future generations.

The 5 is the number of the champion for progression. Your soulful purpose is to institute or initiate a new approach to an old theme—to help people to see things from a different and, perhaps, better perspective. Through a unique concept, idea, business, or creative endeavor, you may change the way things have been done for eons in a specific area of life. A bonus of this purpose number is that it enhances your energy base, which enables you to do all the things you set out to do!

PURPOSE NUMBER 6

LONG-RANGE MISSION: To teach, to instigate, and to help humanitarian causes; to care for home and family, and to be socially responsible.

This is the "cosmic teacher" Purpose number and, therefore, you should feel a strong inclination to help and serve *all living things*, especially those less fortunate than you. You might also try to find a way to influence or teach others to have a greater understanding of, and respect for, all of God's creations—including the earth itself. As a role model of humanitarianism, you should find a way to improve the lives of others—either by being a community volunteer, a teacher, or a committed and loving parent or grandparent.

PURPOSE NUMBER 7

LONG-RANGE MISSION: To impart the vast knowledge you have gathered in a science, an art, a philosophy, or a religion through a creative endeavor.

This is the number of the "educator." You have something to give to the universe, and your soulful mission is to proffer to your fellow humans greater insight and understanding of subject matter that you have collected and mastered during the first 40–45 years of your life. Public speaking, writing books/magazine articles, or teaching in the classroom are a few of the primary means used for achieving this mission.

PURPOSE NUMBER 8

LONG-RANGE MISSION: To lead, direct, initiate, and instigate as a leader or executive, and to help the less fortunate through philanthropy.

Your mission is to be the executive, the director, the chairperson of the board, the supervisor, the tycoon. You can acquire money, power and fame, but your innate, soulful desire will be to use your personal talent and money to help others. Because you are comfortable in a leadership role, it is likely you will do your good deeds from a position of power.

PURPOSE NUMBER 9

LONG-RANGE MISSION: To be a universal humanitarian—a good parent, a good mate, and a good citizen; a philanthropist, a minister, a politician—working for the betterment of mankind.

This is the symbol of the "universal humanitarian." Your mission is to save the world (well, maybe not the *whole* world)—and to become a selfless server of the masses. Many of you who have this Purpose number find a calling in the political, medical, or spiritual/religious arenas as you move into your 50s and beyond.

PURPOSE NUMBER 11

LONG-RANGE MISSION: To help people on the spiritual, psychological, and mental planes. To uplift others with words of wisdom; to listen, offer advice, and help others to move forward on their life's journey.

Illumination, inspiration and leadership are associated with the 11. This is the highest number on the spiritual plane in numerology and offers you the ability to help other people mentally, emotionally, psychologically, and spiritually. You may acquire fame and wealth with this Purpose number, but it is *most* essential that you realize your highest purpose, which is to do something to help others.

PURPOSE NUMBER 22

LONG-RANGE MISSION: To organize and build; to maintain a business enterprise that offers work to others and helps people through service to the community and perhaps the world.

The influence of this Purpose number is that of the Master Builder. It enables you to acquire international fame and acclaim, or the reverence of your peers, through building a solid and practical foundation that offers others a way to achieve their own goals and dreams. You can also succeed as a politician, ambassador, or world leader, as long as your mission focuses on helping your fellow humans.

CHAPTER 8

Narrowing It Down:

Personal Year, Month, Day

There are cycles in everything in the universe and the Personal Year, Month, and Day are your cycles. Your Personal Year gives the big picture view of the influences and outlook of your birthday year. Your Personal Month enables you to focus on different aspects of your life throughout the birthday year. Your Personal Day focuses on the here and now and helps to keep you on a personal self-motivation track.

YOUR PERSONAL YEAR

HOW TO CALCULATE YOUR PERSONAL YEAR

This book bases the Personal Year from birthday to birthday. words, if you were born on June 6, your Personal Year for the current year begins on June 6 and continues through June 5 of the following year.

To find your Personal Year, add the month you were born to the day you were born and reduce that number to a single digit. Then add that number to the Universal Year number for the current year. See specific years below:

2000 = 2	2004 = 6	2008 = 1	2012 = 5	2016 = 9	2020 = 4
2001 = 3	2005 = 7	2009 = 2	2013 = 6	2017 = 1	2021 = 5
2002 = 4	2006 = 8	2010 = 3	2014 = 7	2018 = 2	2022 = 6
2003 = 5	2007 = 7	2011 = 4	2015 = 8	2019 = 3	2023 = 7

Example: For the birth date of June 6, you would add 6 (June) + 6 (day) = 12, and 1 + 2 = 3. To determine the Personal Year for 2001, you would add 3 (the Universal Year number) + 3 = 6. The Personal Year number for the year 2001 for someone born on June 6 is 6.

My Personal Year is: _____

DEFINITIONS OF EACH PERSONAL YEAR FOLLOW

PERSONAL YEAR NUMBER 1

HIGHLIGHT: A major shift in your life and/or your way of viewing life in general.

EMPHASIS: Setting definitive goals, making resolute decisions, taking assertive actions, and flowing with constructive changes that improve your life.

This powerful turning point year sets in motion a whole slew of new experiences, desires, and changes to your life. It is the year of new beginnings—casting out the old and welcoming in the new. Some changes may, in fact, be forced upon you in order to accelerate your personal evolution. Some of you who are more difficult to budge out of your comfort zones may ignore even the strongest signals to change and might simply resolve to do something different with your life at a later time. It's important to acknowledge, however, that this year, being the first year in a nine-year phase, is the most significant year for *planting the seeds* that you want to harvest over the next seven to eight years. And, *it is most* important that you begin now to take the time to write down your future goals. Your timing can be important here, and it is best to write your goals down during the first 52 days after your birthday, as that is the most powerful time of this life-altering year. You must take masterful control of your life during this year and begin to steer it in the direction you want to go. If you don't, before the year is over, you might experience a challenging lesson that is beyond your control. *Believe in your dreams and start the process now that can make them come true!*

AFFIRMATION: I will write down my future goals and keep them in a prominent place to be read and reread throughout this major transition year.

PERSONAL YEAR NUMBER 2

HIGHLIGHT: Nurturing yourself; overcoming feelings of impatience, sensitivity, and irritability.

EMPHASIS: Stop to smell the roses; meditate, exercise (preferably outdoors), practice yoga, read for pleasure, chill.

Now that the seeds have been planted in Personal Year 1, it is time to iron out the kinks in your personal life by doing things that make you feel good. You have just ended a year of action and change, and you may feel impatient, wanting to see some fruits of your labors. However, as you know, anything worthwhile takes time to evolve and to grow; so relax, kick back, be patient, and focus your energies on nurturing yourself, your family, and your friends. It is not a time to think only of yourself, but it is essential that you take some time out—to enjoy nature, meditate, read your favorite novels, and take some time to stop and smell the flowers. If you do not follow this advice, your unsettled nature may cause you and everyone around you to suffer needlessly. The vibration of this year can cause moodiness and feelings of dissatisfaction and discontent. Many marriages and other long-term relationships struggle under its influence. It's time to give pause and *be grateful for what you have* (and stop complaining about what you don't have) and, most definitely, continue working toward your goals!

AFFIRMATION: I will be nurturing to myself and others, and I will practice being grateful.

PERSONAL YEAR NUMBER 3

HIGHLIGHT: Giving to yourself and others with enthusiasm and joy!

EMPHASIS: Being social, entertaining family and friends, going on expeditions and adventures, taking the trip of your dreams, getting married, getting divorced; doing something just for you that makes you feel especially good!

The highlight and emphasis of this year may seem like a continuation of last year, but they are not. Under this year's influence, you will *feel more* like socializing, having fun, and doing nice things for yourself. No matter how difficult the circumstances in your life may be, it is time to use whatever resources you have to give yourself a "joy-generating" experience. You may not be able to take the trip of your dreams, but there may be personal things you can alter that will make you happier. You might even change your career in a way that gives you something more to look forward to every workday. You should see a "sprout" of success this year from the seeds you planted in Personal Year 1. Over the course of the past two years, you may have experienced changes that have given your life a different focus. Realize that all the readjusting and refining you do with your life are passages that can lead to a better you—if you are willing to see them that way. So, this is the year to celebrate your progress and your growth! Say Yes! to life, and then go out and have some fun!

AFFIRMATION: Every day, I will make joy and happiness a priority in my life.

PERSONAL YEAR NUMBER 4

HIGHLIGHT: The establishment of a secure and stable foundation to ensure your goals are achieved.

EMPHASIS: Steering your goal plan on a steady course; brining order, consistency, and dedication to your goal efforts.

By this time, your "garden of goals" should be showing some major signs of life—and besides the goals you've set for yourself, there may be others that need your immediate attention. This is the year to *weed out any undesirable growth*. If you are having financial problems, it's time to fix that area of your life. Budgeting and altering negative spending habits falls under this year's influence. If you have other personal habits that are hindering your ability to be at your best, now is the time to tackle them, too. Viewing your life, career, and lifestyle with greater objectivity can help you to find ways to alter your attitude and other circumstances for the better. You may feel restricted and lack the enthusiasm to forge forward, but if you make an effort through hard work, determination, perseverance, and using common sense, one or more of your ultimate desires and goals may begin to manifest itself. A good motto for this Personal Year is the affirmation written in the book "Think and Grow Rich" by Napoleon Hill: "*If you can conceive and believe, you can achieve!*"

AFFIRMATION: I will concentrate on weeding out the negative aspects of my life! I will continue to work on and believe in my dreams and goals!

PERSONAL YEAR NUMBER 5

HIGHLIGHT: Effecting a major change that promotes greater freedom, expansion, and growth.

EMPHASIS: Forming new relationships, eliciting new opportunities, feeling adventurous and willing to take risks, and inviting progressive movement into your life.

If it feels like everything's in motion, it is. Whether it's the way you're feeling emotionally, or an actual physical event, everything in your life is in transition, and what's moving is YOU! The movement may involve changing where you live or where you work, a change in one of your relationships or family, or a change in yourself. After all the weeding out and persevering of last year, it is now time to proclaim, promote, publicize, and advertise your garden of life—namely your goals! This is the second most powerful turning point year in the nine-year phase. Regardless of whether you are prepared to move forward or not at this time, your life's circumstances may have a way of forcing the issue before this year is over. Go with the flow and accept whatever comes your way or, better yet, take the reigns in your own hands and steer the course of your life yourself! Energy and an optimistic attitude are two of the greatest blessings associated with this powerful influence. You should feel the motivation and drive to carry you to a new level in your goal plan. Your enthusiasm and optimism will inspire you to have confidence in yourself and to really believe that you will achieve your dreams!

AFFIRMATION: By enthusiastically accepting and welcoming change, I will realize personal evolution and advancement of my goals.

PERSONAL YEAR NUMBER 6

HIGHLIGHT: A positive change in your home and family; establishing new friendships and love relations.

EMPHASIS: Being responsible to home, family members, love relationships, and friendships.

You've made it through the *spin* year of singing your own praises and making dramatic life changes, and now it's time to concentrate your energies on the home front. If you're single, this could be the year you meet your matrimonial match. If you've already found Mr./Ms. Right, a 6 year's the perfect Personal Year for marriage. Or, you might end a close personal relationship that you know just isn't working. If you are married, you may be preparing for a new addition to the family, changing the location of your home, or making major purchases for your home. If you have teens, you may experience a year of wrestling with their needs and dealing with your and their frustrations. Or, you may become a grandparent for the first time (if you have kids that old). The 6 is the number of humanitarianism and caring for all things of the earth, so even your pets and plants fall under its influence. Fundamentally, it's a time *to be loving, understanding, compassionate, caring, and kind to everyone*, especially to those you love the most.

AFFIRMATION: I will be more responsible, understanding, and loving this year.

PERSONAL YEAR NUMBER 7

HIGHLIGHT: Determining, through introspection, contemplation and meditation, the most effective course to reach your ultimate goals and dreams.

EMPHASIS: Researching, analyzing, reflecting, and meditating to gain the greatest understanding of your ultimate desires and goals.

This year's influence promotes the need for you to spend some time alone contemplating your life. It's a time when you may ask yourself, "Where am I going?" "What am I supposed to be doing?" "Is this all there will be to my life?" You may find yourself doing some serious thinking and major soul-searching as you ponder the choices you've made and reflect on your life, yourself, and your career. It's as though you are scrutinizing your life by shaking up a bottle of liquid and, once the residue settles, you'll be able to recognize the answers to all your questions. Imagining, learning through research, deliberating, and analyzing will help you with this clarifying process. This is not a good time to make changes, to form partnerships, or to do anything else that requires commitment and definitive action. Like Personal Year 2, patience will be one of the most crucial attributes you can possess. By the close of this question-filled year, you will more than likely make a concrete decision about your future.

AFFIRMATION: I will practice patience and give myself some quiet time to ruminate about my life and future.

PERSONAL YEAR NUMBER 8

HIGHLIGHT: You will enjoy the harvest of all the labor and effort you have put forth in the past seven years!

EMPHASIS: Taking the actions, making the requests, and being wholly self-confident that you deserve to obtain one or more of your most desired goals and/or fondest dreams.

This is the most telltale year of the nine-year phase. The benefits, honors, praise, salary raises, and/or goal achievements you gain this year will be in direct proportion to how hard you have worked toward your goals and personal growth over the past seven years. This is the year you reap what you have sown. Will your "garden of life" bear a bountiful harvest, or yield only a paltry reward? This is also a year that promises the greatest advances and achievement by your taking diligent action and making responsible decisions. You can sell something and get a higher payment than expected, or you might purchase something for a very good price. This influence grants you the ability to ask for more and get more. It is the most profit-making and remunerative year of all! If you have been wanting to change your career, this is the year to do so. If you are thinking of moving, the prospects of gain through such a move are higher than ever before. Starting a business, entering into a partnership, or taking any other kind of calculated risk are favored under this materially-gratifying vibration. Competency, consistency and prudence, along with integrity, industriousness and courage, are the most necessary components for attaining the greatest potential from this year's charge. *Take a giant step toward your most haughty goal. Lady luck is in your corner until your next birthday!*

AFFIRMATION: I will take action to actualize my dreams and goals now, and my efforts will bring forth bountiful returns!

PERSONAL YEAR NUMBER 9

HIGHLIGHTS: Closing up shop, finishing off projects, and ending a whole phase of your life.

EMPHASIS: Cleaning out the attics of your life, the mental, philosophical, personal, and physical. Moving out, leaving behind, breaking up, casting off, and removing all things that hinder or curtail the path to your ultimate goals, hopes and dreams.

Most people who enter Personal Year 9 feel some degree of discomfort and yet are incapable of figuring out what is causing those feelings. That's because this year's overtone is one of closing down, shutting off, and dismantling. In a manner of speaking, your eight-year growth cycle has come to and end, and the garden you have planted needs a little TLC to get ready for the next season. Because it is a year of endings, it is not a good time to get married, start a business, or take any other kind of action that you hope will have some permanence in your life. However, if you marry in a Personal Year 9, but met your mate and planned the marriage in any previous year, it is likely that your marriage will endure. It's the things that are *started* in the Personal Year 9 that seem to be fleeting. The most important action you can take this year is to rid yourself of the people and things that are no longer pose a positive influence in your life. The 9 also represents aristocracy and gentility, compassion and philanthropy and you may, therefore, become involved in charitable work or be honored for a philanthropic gesture. In fact, when your energy is low (and it will be during the majority of this year), it might be good for you to get involved in activities that help others. Giving selflessly is a sure-fire way to cure what ails you, especially this year!

AFFIRMATION: I will rid myself of the influences that do not bring me pleasure and happiness and give generously of myself to people in need and humanitarian causes throughout the year.

YOUR PERSONAL MONTH

To find your Personal Month, add your Personal Year number to the number of the month. For example, for a June 6 birthday, the Personal Month for August 2001 is 5, (6 [personal year] + 8 [August] = 14, and 1 + 4 = 5).

DEFINITIONS OF EACH PERSONAL MONTH FOLLOW

PERSONAL MONTH NUMBER 1

Be bold, confident, and assertive for the power of the Sun, the ruler of the 1, is your energy generator this month. Initiate something new, create something original, set an ambitious goal, resolve to be a winner. This is the month to plant the seeds of new beginnings, to take charge, to lead, and to forge forward! It's a time for *action*! The torch has been passed to you, so run with all your might toward your hopes and dreams. There's no time like *now*!

PERSONAL MONTH NUMBER 2

Be adaptable, cooperative, considerate, and understanding. That's a lot to ask for a whole month but it's the best advice to offer considering the sensitivity-provoking and emotion-evoking influence of the 2. Patience is the antidote for the things that irritate you, and unfortunately you may find that your supply is at an all-time low. Try not to push, cajole, or force anything to go you way. This is the month to let go and let the powers of the universe work for you. The seeds of last month's actions are germinating, so *relax* and let things happen.

PERSONAL MONTH NUMBER 3

Now is the time to break out the music and get up and boogie. This is the month of celebration, even if to you that means just plain kicking back in a hammock. You've taken action in the Year 1, been patient (hopefully) in the Year 2, and now you should congratulate yourself and let the good times roll. Go on a vacation, do something you've always wanted to do, or spend some time exercising your right brain through creative endeavors or just plain daydreaming. Do whatever pleases your soul the most, and start doing it *now!*

PERSONAL MONTH NUMBER 4

All play and no work makes for chaos! Now that the "fun" month has passed, it's time to get out those tools because there's some maintenance that needs to be done in your garden of life. It's time to take stock of all the areas of your life that require order, planning, and practical attention. Budgeting, organizing, constructing, and categorizing are all appropriate and worthwhile activities. Forming partnerships, either in business or in love, also fall under this vibration but, primarily, it's time to get all your ducks in a row because big changes may be coming your way next month! *Get prepared!*

PERSONAL MONTH NUMBER 5

Once the best-laid plans have been made, it's time to make some constructive changes. Promotion, moving, expanding your world, and venturing out are essential to your personal growth at this time. Watch for opportunities that arise that may bump you out of your comfort zone and help push you up a rung on the achievement scale. Don't procrastinate! The positive actions you take this month or the significant changes you make, will have a great impact on your immediate future!

PERSONAL MONTH NUMBER 6

The highest expression of this month's vibration is to put others' needs before your own and to be kind, loving, and responsible. You may need to pay extra special attention to circumstances at home or with your family and friends. You may alter your home in some way, or you may be moving. There may be family issues that need to be dealt with, or there may be the need (or the opportunity) to spend more time with friends or family members. If you're married, you may feel particularly romantic and loving toward your mate. If you're single, you may meet Mr./Ms. Right or solidify an existing relationship. Negative feelings can crop up under this vibration, too, and sometimes relationships that have not been working well come to an end during a 6 month.

You will benefit most by being kind, caring, and compassionate to one and all!

PERSONAL MONTH NUMBER 7

This month's vibration advocates the need for you to shut down, to cool your jets, or just to be quiet and contemplative for a while. The 7 is associated with learning, researching, analyzing, and being introspective. If you act out the IBM motto—think, think, think—you will be making the right connection with this penetrating vibration. This is a good time to bring some balance to the physical, emotional, and spiritual aspects of your life, too. Meditation and yoga are excellent practices to do under this influence. You may feel very restless and find it difficult to be reflective and peaceful, but some of those feelings may be exactly why it is right for you to take some quiet *time out*—now!

PERSONAL MONTH NUMBER 8

This is the month of accomplishment and rewards. It is a time when you will feel greater self-confidence and the ambition to go after whatever you want. If you've been wanting to ask for a raise, or you've been thinking about selling or buying something, now is the time to do so. The 8 is associated with money, power, and fame and, depending on your past efforts, you may be in store for one or more of those gains. The influence of the 8 rewards in direct relation to the energy expended. If you are industrious and your motives are honest and principled, you can expect to receive the largest rewards for your efforts. If you act otherwise, you can expect much less in return. You must give a lot of thought to your choices and inducements at this time.

PERSONAL MONTH NUMBER 9

Aspects of your life that are closing out, finishing off and ending up fall under this month's vibration. It is not a time to try something new, or form a new relationship—either business or personal—because anything started under the 9 vibration usually doesn't have much staying power. The 9 also advocates humanitarian activities and selfless service to others. Its influence can bring about circumstances that cause you to experience humility or a greater understanding of and compassion for others. Do not resist any opportunity to help and serve others at this time, and you will definitely benefit from your actions.

YOUR PERSONAL DAY

To calculate your Personal Day, add the number of your Personal Month to the day of the month in question. Example: Birth date: June 6. The Personal Year for 2001 is 6; the Personal Month for August is 5, and the Personal Day for August 8 is 4 (5 [Personal Month] + 8 [day of month] = 13, and 1 + 3 = 4).

DEFINITIONS OF EACH PERSONAL DAY FOLLOW

PERSONAL DAY NUMBER 1

ACTION DAY. Be bold, commanding, and even demanding today. The overtone of this day grants you the opportunity for new beginnings, so take a calculated risk. Do things that make you feel more self-confident and more in charge of your own fate. Make decisions. Trust that your definitive actions will deliver the results you desire. This is a powerful, turning point day, so put it to good use!

PERSONAL DAY NUMBER 2

SELF-NURTURING DAY. Be good to yourself. Improve your diet, get some well-needed rest, take a long bath, do some enjoyment reading, start yoga classes, exercise outdoors, and/or get together with friends. In general, do things that give you a sense of well-being. The importance of this day is to cultivate better personal health and vitality.

PERSONAL DAY NUMBER 3

EXPRESS YOURSELF DAY. Put on your most colorful outfit and wear a smile because this is a day to celebrate life! Do things that are fun and creative. Enjoy the company of good friends and your family. Have a good laugh and enthusiastically spread good feelings wherever you go. Deliver honest and deserving compliments at random. You may even experience some unexpected good fortune on this delight-filled day. Be happy!

PERSONAL DAY NUMBER 4

PRACTICAL AND STABILIZING DAY. Do whatever is required to make your life run smoother today. Budget, balance, organize, plan, and complete unfinished business. Give greater attention to all the details in your life that need to be straightened up, cleaned out, systematized, and finalized. Be productive, law-abiding, cool-headed, and deliberate in your actions, and you will be glad you were!

PERSONAL DAY NUMBER 5

A DAY OF CHANGE. Use this day to expand your horizons and further the progress of your hopes and dreams. Be spontaneous and confident. Promote, advertise, and enthusiastically express your ideas and interests to those who can help you move forward. Be spontaneous. Change your hair, clothes, or entire lifestyle to fit more appropriately with your goals. Mainly, continue advancing toward your highest self!

PERSONAL DAY NUMBER 6

A DAY OF LOVE AND RESPONSIBILITY. This is a day to make friends, family members, and the home front a priority. Relationships with co-workers may need some attention, too. Be especially kind, loving, and nurturing to people in need, animals, and all of nature. Listen and practice patience, understanding and tolerance, and be prepared to receive back what you are giving out!

PERSONAL DAY NUMBER 7

A DAY OF INTROSPECTION. Go to your favorite quiet place to be alone for a while and rev up your energy level. Spend time with your thoughts; reflect, and contemplate your life and goals. This break-time helps your psyche to solve all your worldly problems and frustrations. You may also use this time to research and analyze selected subject matter or to delve into the mysteries of life. Metaphysical studies, practicing yoga, prayer, or meditation are all excellent ways to experience this day.

PERSONAL DAY NUMBER 8

POWER DAY. Pull out all stops and charge onward and upward! This is the day to ask for more and to receive it. Request a big raise and get it; pitch a concept or idea and have it accepted; take a calculated risk and win! Don't be foolhardy, however. Prudence, honesty, and attention to detail are the keys to the success you will garner on this personal advancement day.

PERSONAL DAY NUMBER 9

A DAY OF ENDINGS, BEING COMPASSIONATE, AND GIVING. This influence may bring something to an end or some aspect of your life may come to a close today. Endings bring new beginnings (tomorrow is a new beginnings day), so don't waste time regretting anything or worrying about something that's done with and over. This is also a day to give selflessly, or to do something that is solely for others, and to reap the benefit of a joyful soul!

CHAPTER 9

Coloring Your Life with Numbers
and
the Wizard's Star

WHAT IS THE WIZARD'S STAR?

The Wizard's Star is a symbol, in vivid color, of your individuality. It is very rare to find any two Wizard's Stars that are exactly alike because the colors are assigned by the numbers derived from your birth date and birth name. It is intended to give the reader an image of inspiration and to provide motivation to live up to the wonderful qualities and potential associated with each of the six numbers and colors that comprise your Wizard's Star. (Note: You must determine your Personality, Destiny, Character, Soul Urge, and Hidden Agenda numbers before you can compose your star. See Chapters 4 and 5.)

THE HISTORY OF THE WIZARD'S STAR

The Wizard's Star (referred to in ancient times as the Wizard's Foot) is a five-pointed star comprised of three triangles that was designed by philosopher/mathematician Pythagoras. According to the folklore, the Phythagorean followers used this star for health purposes. Its powers were believed to effect positive health conditions and healing. It was also used by the masses of those ancient times to ward off misfortune and the Evil Eye and replicas of it were placed over doorways and on bedsteads for that purpose. There is a passage in Geothe's Mephistopheles that has the Devil saying:

"My steps by one slight obstacle are controlled—by the Wizard's Foot that is on your threshold."

HOW THE COLORS WERE ASSIGNED

Pythagoras is credited with assigning colors to each of the primary numbers. Seven of the colors are associated with seven chakra points in the body. The author has assigned colors to numbers 5, 8, 9 and 22, as follows:

1 = red
Red is the color of the base chakra, which governs primal instincts.

2 = orange
Orange is the color of the pelvic chakra, which governs sensuality.

3 = yellow
Yellow is the color of the solar plexus chakra, which governs emotions.

4 = green
Green is the color of the heart chakra, and it governs feelings of love.

5= turquoise
Turquoise is the color of the thymus which is associated with perceptivity.

6 = blue
Blue is the color of the throat chakra, and governs speech.

7 = purple
Purple is the color of the third eye chakra, and it governs intuition.

8 = fuchsia
Fuchsia governs your ability to transcend the three-dimensional state through use of the imagination and dreams.

9 = marigold
Marigold represents innate (old soul) wisdom.

11 = violet
Violet is the color of the crown chakra, which is associated with spiritual sensitivities.

22 = Indigo

Indigo blue is the color of the Master Builder and represents high-minded aspirations.

The 11 and 22, the two primary Master numbers in numerology, are the Master "giver" numbers, in their most positive expression. Having a Master number doesn't make you any more special than someone without Master numbers. The Master numbers are definitely considered elevated in the science of numerology, but that elevation is based on a spiritual philosophy that portends, "the more you are given, the more you must give." Most people who are in tune with their Master number vibrations feel impelled to contribute to the betterment of society and mankind. Numerous others who have these numbers find it difficult to live up to the high vibration, which includes high standards and morals, that these numbers require in order to manifest their greatest potential and power. In those cases, the 11 and 22 are lived as their base numbers of 2 (1 + 1 = 2) and 4 (2 + 2 = 4).

HOW IT WORKS

Once you have calculated the six primary numbers of your numerology profile, you are equipped to make your own Wizard's Star. In the back folder of the book, you will find sheets of Wizard's Stars [see Wizard's Star worksheets in the back of the book].

Lay the sheet with the Wizard's Star on a flat surface. Using a black marker pen, write your Destiny number in the center pentagram of the star. Then write in the numbers that correlate with each of the star points. Color each point and the pentagram according to the color chart. Once you have completed your Wizard's Star, you may find it interesting and enlightening to make the Wizard's Stars of your family members and friends as well.

SUMMARY OF THE SIX PRIMARY NUMBERS

A brief summary of how the six primary numbers apply to the character and surroundings is as follows:

1. The Destiny number (the small center star) defines who you gravitate toward as friends and mates, what you came to accomplish in this life, where you like to go for fun and recreation, how you act and react to your surroundings, and why you like what you like—from social to career interests.

2. The Personality number (lower left point of the star) defines the "real" you—your private (inside) self.

3. The Attitude number (lower right point of the star) defines your sentiment, perception, and temperament toward people, places, and things—especially in your first 30 years of life.

4. The Character number (top center point of the star), the strongest vibration of your public (outside) self.

5. The Soul Urge number (top left point of the star) is your soul's driving force.

6. The Hidden Agenda (top right point of the star) is the secret or hidden desire of the public self and the Soul Urge.

WIZARD'S STAR PROFILES OF FAMOUS PEOPLE

Following are 16 Wizard's Star Profiles including those for:

Christina Aguilera, Madonna, Mohammed Ali, Salvador Dali, Albert Einstein, Bill Gates, John Lennon, Tom Cruise, Ricky Martin, Elvis Presley, Princess Diana, Barbara Streisand, Elizabeth Taylor, Venus Williams, Oprah Winfrey, and Tiger Woods.

Wizard's Star
Christina Aguilera
Birth Date: 12/18/80

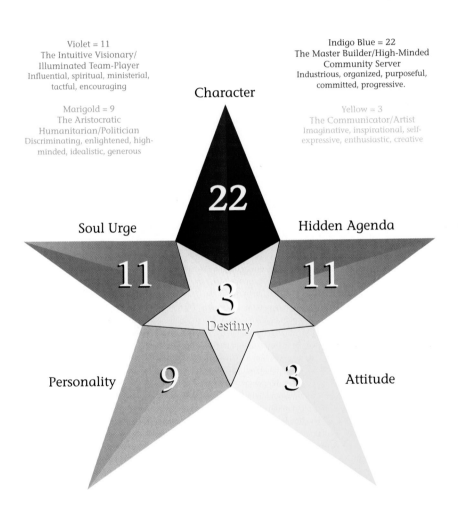

Violet = 11
The Intuitive Visionary/
Illuminated Team-Player
Influential, spiritual, ministerial,
tactful, encouraging

Marigold = 9
The Aristocratic
Humanitarian/Politician
Discriminating, enlightened, high-
minded, idealistic, generous

Indigo Blue = 22
The Master Builder/High-Minded
Community Server
Industrious, organized, purposeful,
committed, progressive.

Yellow = 3
The Communicator/Artist
Imaginative, inspirational, self-
expressive, enthusiastic, creative

Character

22

Soul Urge

Hidden Agenda

11

11

3
Destiny

Personality

9

3

Attitude

Wizard's Star
Madonna Louise Veronica Ciccone
Birth Date: 8/16/58

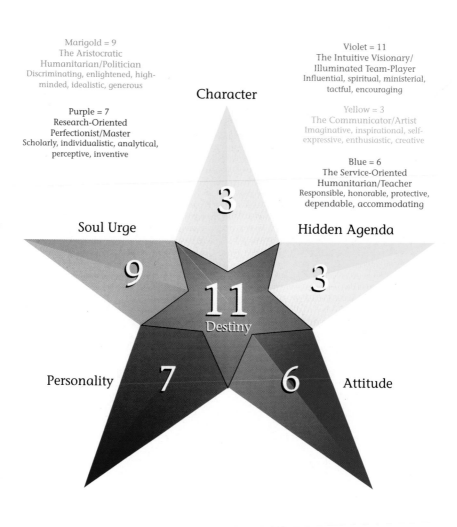

Marigold = 9
The Aristocratic
Humanitarian/Politician
Discriminating, enlightened, high-
minded, idealistic, generous

Purple = 7
Research-Oriented
Perfectionist/Master
Scholarly, individualistic, analytical,
perceptive, inventive

Violet = 11
The Intuitive Visionary/
Illuminated Team-Player
Influential, spiritual, ministerial,
tactful, encouraging

Yellow = 3
The Communicator/Artist
Imaginative, inspirational, self-
expressive, enthusiastic, creative

Blue = 6
The Service-Oriented
Humanitarian/Teacher
Responsible, honorable, protective,
dependable, accommodating

Character

Soul Urge

Hidden Agenda

3

9

3

11
Destiny

Personality

7

6

Attitude

Wizard's Star
Cassius Marcellus Clay
(Mohammed Ali)
Birth Date: 1/17/42

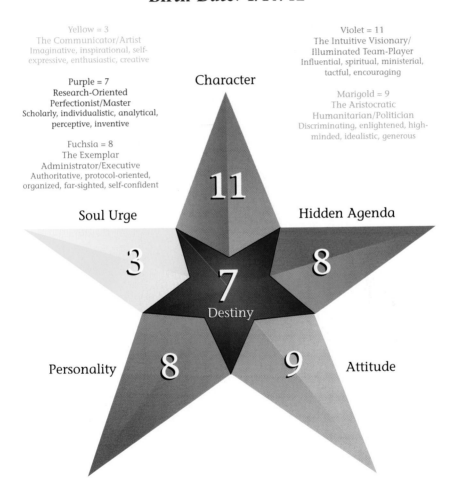

Yellow = 3
The Communicator/Artist
Imaginative, inspirational, self-
expressive, enthusiastic, creative

Purple = 7
Research-Oriented
Perfectionist/Master
Scholarly, individualistic, analytical,
perceptive, inventive

Fuchsia = 8
The Exemplar
Administrator/Executive
Authoritative, protocol-oriented,
organized, far-sighted, self-confident

Violet = 11
The Intuitive Visionary/
Illuminated Team-Player
Influential, spiritual, ministerial,
tactful, encouraging

Marigold = 9
The Aristocratic
Humanitarian/Politician
Discriminating, enlightened, high-
minded, idealistic, generous

Character

Soul Urge

Hidden Agenda

11

3

7
Destiny

8

Personality

8

9

Attitude

Wizard's Star
Salvador Dali
Birth Date: 5/11/04

Marigold = 9
The Aristocratic
Humanitarian/Politician
Discriminating, enlightened, high-
minded, idealistic, generous

Violet = 11
The Intuitive Visionary/
Illuminated Team-Player
Influential, spiritual, ministerial,
tactful, encouraging

Yellow = 3
The Communicator/Artist
Imaginative, inspirational, self-
expressive, enthusiastic, creative

Red = 1
The Individualist/Leader
Original, ambitious, dynamic,
innovative, self-confident

Purple = 7
Research-Oriented
Perfectionist/Master
Scholarly, individualistic, analytical,
perceptive, inventive

Character

Soul Urge

Hidden Agenda

1

9

1

3
Destiny

Personality

11

7

Attitude

Wizard's Star
Albert Einstein
Birth Date: 3/14/1879

Purple = 7
Research-Oriented
Perfectionist/Master
Scholarly, individualistic, analytical,
perceptive, inventive

Turquoise = 5
The Freedom-Seeking Go-Getter
Energetic, adaptable, inquisitive,
independent, non-conformist

Blue = 6
The Service-Oriented
Humanitarian/Teacher
Responsible, honorable, protective,
dependable, accommodating

Marigold = 9
The Aristocratic
Humanitarian/Politician
Discriminating, enlightened, high-
minded, idealistic, generous

Violet = 11
The Intuitive Visionary/
Illuminated Team-Player
Influential, spiritual, ministerial,
tactful, encouraging

Fuchsia = 8
The Exemplar
Administrator/Executive
Authoritative, protocol-oriented,
organized, far-sighted, self-confident

Character

Soul Urge

Hidden Agenda

Personality

Attitude

9

7

11

6
Destiny

5

8

Wizard's Star
William Henry Gates
Birth Date: 10/28/55

Indigo Blue = 22
The Master Builder/High-Minded
Community Server
Industrious, organized, purposeful,
committed, progressive.

Yellow = 3
The Communicator/Artist
Imaginative, inspirational, self-
expressive, enthusiastic, creative

Red = 1
The Individualist/Leader
Original, ambitious, dynamic,
innovative, self-confident

Violet = 11
The Intuitive Visionary/
Illuminated Team-Player
Influential, spiritual, ministerial,
tactful, encouraging

Character

Soul Urge

Hidden Agenda

3

1

11

22
Destiny

Personality

1

11

Attitude

Wizard's Star
John Winston Lennon
Birth Date: 10/9/40

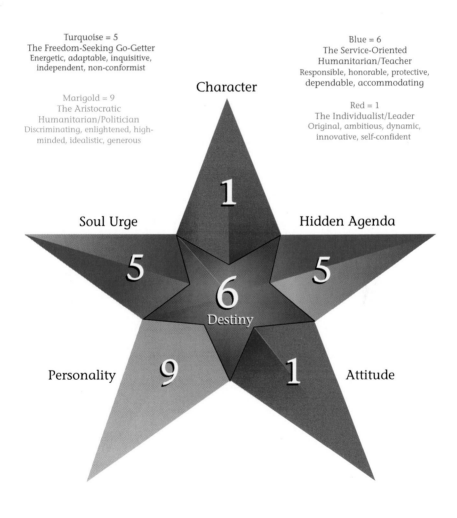

Turquoise = 5
The Freedom-Seeking Go-Getter
Energetic, adaptable, inquisitive,
independent, non-conformist

Blue = 6
The Service-Oriented
Humanitarian/Teacher
Responsible, honorable, protective,
dependable, accommodating

Marigold = 9
The Aristocratic
Humanitarian/Politician
Discriminating, enlightened, high-
minded, idealistic, generous

Red = 1
The Individualist/Leader
Original, ambitious, dynamic,
innovative, self-confident

Character

Soul Urge

Hidden Agenda

1

5

6
Destiny

5

Personality

9

1

Attitude

Wizard's Star
Thomas Cruise Mapother IV
Birth Date: 7/3/62

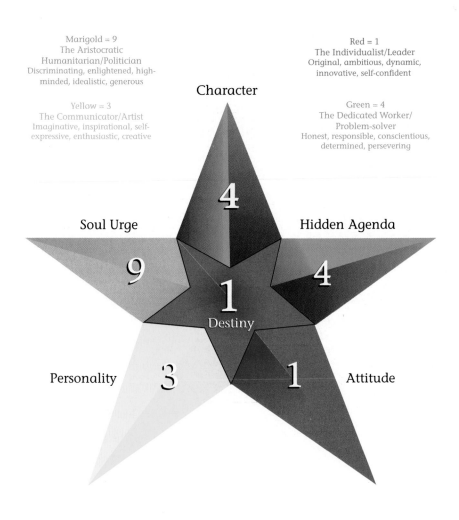

Marigold = 9
The Aristocratic
Humanitarian/Politician
Discriminating, enlightened, high-
minded, idealistic, generous

Yellow = 3
The Communicator/Artist
Imaginative, inspirational, self-
expressive, enthusiastic, creative

Red = 1
The Individualist/Leader
Original, ambitious, dynamic,
innovative, self-confident

Green = 4
The Dedicated Worker/
Problem-solver
Honest, responsible, conscientious,
determined, persevering

Character

Soul Urge

Hidden Agenda

4

9

1
Destiny

4

Personality

3

1

Attitude

Wizard's Star
Enrique Jose Martin Morales IV
(Ricky Martin)
Birth Date: 12/24/71

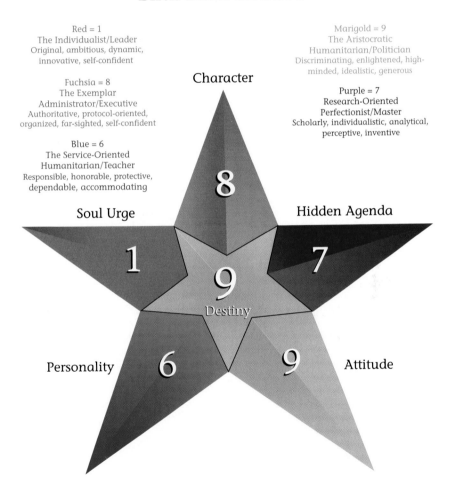

Red = 1
The Individualist/Leader
Original, ambitious, dynamic,
innovative, self-confident

Fuchsia = 8
The Exemplar
Administrator/Executive
Authoritative, protocol-oriented,
organized, far-sighted, self-confident

Blue = 6
The Service-Oriented
Humanitarian/Teacher
Responsible, honorable, protective,
dependable, accommodating

Marigold = 9
The Aristocratic
Humanitarian/Politician
Discriminating, enlightened, high-
minded, idealistic, generous

Purple = 7
Research-Oriented
Perfectionist/Master
Scholarly, individualistic, analytical,
perceptive, inventive

Character

Soul Urge

Hidden Agenda

8

1

9
Destiny

7

Personality

6

9

Attitude

Wizard's Star
Elvis Aaron Presley
Birth Date: 1/8/35

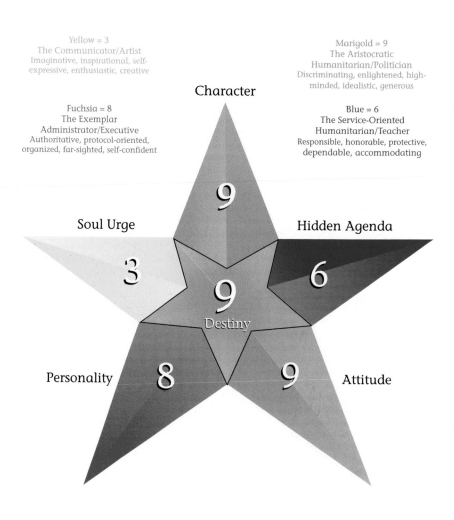

Yellow = 3
The Communicator/Artist
Imaginative, inspirational, self-
expressive, enthusiastic, creative

Marigold = 9
The Aristocratic
Humanitarian/Politician
Discriminating, enlightened, high-
minded, idealistic, generous

Fuchsia = 8
The Exemplar
Administrator/Executive
Authoritative, protocol-oriented,
organized, far-sighted, self-confident

Blue = 6
The Service-Oriented
Humanitarian/Teacher
Responsible, honorable, protective,
dependable, accommodating

Character

Soul Urge

Hidden Agenda

9

3

9

6

Destiny

Personality

8

9

Attitude

Wizard's Star
Lady Diana Frances Spencer
Birth Date: 7/1/61

Red = 1
The Individualist/Leader
Original, ambitious, dynamic,
innovative, self-confident

Violet = 11
The Intuitive Visionary/
Illuminated Team-Player
Influential, spiritual, ministerial,
tactful, encouraging

Fuchsia = 8
The Exemplar
Administrator/Executive
Authoritative, protocol-oriented,
organized, far-sighted, self-confident

Purple = 7
Research-Oriented
Perfectionist/Master
Scholarly, individualistic, analytical,
perceptive, inventive

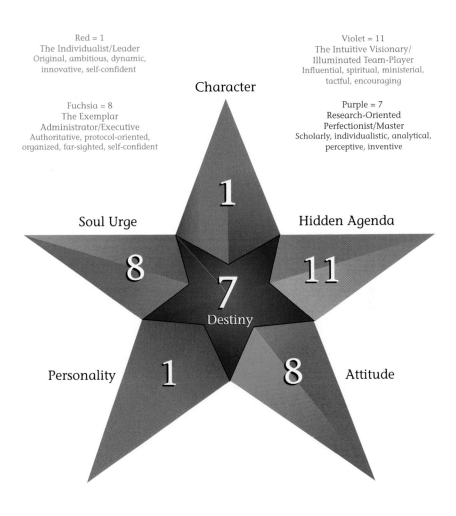

Character

Soul Urge

Hidden Agenda

1

8

11

7
Destiny

Personality

1

8

Attitude

Wizard's Star
Barbara Joan Streisand
(Barbra)
Birth Date: 4/24/42

Purple = 7
Research-Oriented
Perfectionist/Master
Scholarly, individualistic, analytical,
perceptive, inventive

Yellow = 3
The Communicator/Artist
Imaginative, inspirational, self-
expressive, enthusiastic, creative

Fuchsia = 8
The Exemplar
Administrator/Executive
Authoritative, protocol-oriented,
organized, far-sighted, self-confident

Turquoise = 5
The Freedom-Seeking Go-Getter
Energetic, adaptable, inquisitive,
independent, non-conformist

Blue = 6
The Service-Oriented
Humanitarian/Teacher
Responsible, honorable, protective,
dependable, accommodating

Red = 1
The Individualist/Leader
Original, ambitious, dynamic,
innovative, self-confident

Wizard's Star
Elizabeth Rosemond Taylor
Birth Date: 2/27/32

Blue = 6
The Service-Oriented
Humanitarian/Teacher
Responsible, honorable, protective,
dependable, accommodating

Marigold = 9
The Aristocratic
Humanitarian/Politician
Discriminating, enlightened, high-
minded, idealistic, generous

Yellow = 3
The Communicator/Artist
Imaginative, inspirational, self-
expressive, enthusiastic, creative

Fuchsia = 8
The Exemplar
Administrator/Executive
Authoritative, protocol-oriented,
organized, far-sighted, self-confident

Violet = 11
The Intuitive Visionary/
Illuminated Team-Player
Influential, spiritual, ministerial,
tactful, encouraging

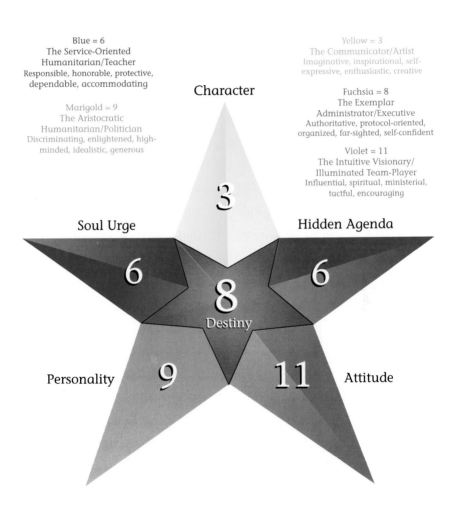

Character

Soul Urge

Hidden Agenda

3

6

8
Destiny

6

Personality

9

11

Attitude

Wizard's Star
Venus Ebone Starr Williams
Birth Date: 6/17/80

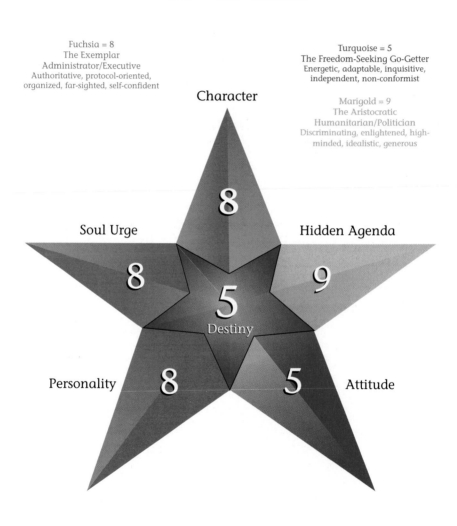

Fuchsia = 8
The Exemplar
Administrator/Executive
Authoritative, protocol-oriented,
organized, far-sighted, self-confident

Turquoise = 5
The Freedom-Seeking Go-Getter
Energetic, adaptable, inquisitive,
independent, non-conformist

Marigold = 9
The Aristocratic
Humanitarian/Politician
Discriminating, enlightened, high-
minded, idealistic, generous

Character

Soul Urge

Hidden Agenda

Destiny

Personality

Attitude

Wizard's Star
Oprah Gail Winfrey
Birth Date: 1/29/54

Indigo Blue = 22
The Master Builder/High-Minded
Community Server
Industrious, organized, purposeful,
committed, progressive.

Violet = 11
The Intuitive Visionary/
Illuminated Team-Player
Influential, spiritual, ministerial,
tactful, encouraging

Purple = 7
Research-Oriented
Perfectionist/Master
Scholarly, individualistic, analytical,
perceptive, inventive

Turquoise = 5
The Freedom-Seeking Go-Getter
Energetic, adaptable, inquisitive,
independent, non-conformist

Yellow = 3
The Communicator/Artist
Imaginative, inspirational, self-
expressive, enthusiastic, creative

Character

7

Soul Urge

Hidden Agenda

11

5

22
Destiny

Personality

11

3

Attitude

Wizard's Star
Eldrick Woods
(Tiger)
Birth Date: 12/30/75

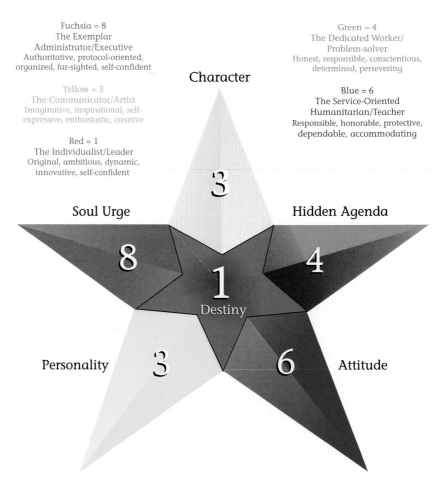

Fuchsia = 8
The Exemplar
Administrator/Executive
Authoritative, protocol-oriented,
organized, far-sighted, self-confident

Yellow = 3
The Communicator/Artist
Imaginative, inspirational, self-
expressive, enthusiastic, creative

Red = 1
The Individualist/Leader
Original, ambitious, dynamic,
innovative, self-confident

Green = 4
The Dedicated Worker/
Problem-solver
Honest, responsible, conscientious,
determined, persevering

Blue = 6
The Service-Oriented
Humanitarian/Teacher
Responsible, honorable, protective,
dependable, accommodating

Character

Soul Urge

Hidden Agenda

8

3

1
Destiny

4

Personality

3

6

Attitude

Chapter 10
Relationships and Compatibility

There are many factors that affect compatibility, from how personally content someone is, to how much money they may have in the bank, to the planetary placements in their astrological charts. The following charts are not wholly conclusive guides to compatibility, so don't be too disturbed if you and your mate don't end up with a score as high as you would hope. However, if you take the time to read the definitions of the numbers associated with each person, you may begin to understand some of the reasons why your have or have not been able to get along with one another. This author has used the following method for determining the compatibility of hundreds of clients' life mates, children, mothers, fathers, sisters, brothers, bosses, co-workers, friends, and even family pets when the birthday was available.

A positive compatibility score of the Destiny numbers of two people is very significant because the Destiny number influences how one acclimates to his/her surroundings and the people and things in those surroundings. The Destiny number evokes different responses than the Personality and Character numbers, and that is why there are two different compatibility charts—one for the Destiny number, exclusively, and the other for "All the Other Numbers."

The Score Charts that follow Charts I and II enable you to calculate a bottom-line compatibility rating of the Destiny, Personality, Attitude, Character, Soul Urge, and Hidden Agenda of yourself and another person, or any other couple you might want to analyze from a compatibility standpoint.

NOTE: You must calculate the numbers for each person you're analyzing and write them down so you can refer to them easily before you begin using the following compatibility charts.

CHART I

DESTINY NUMBER COMPATIBILITY

PERSON #2	PERSON #1 (D=Destiny Number)										
	D-1	D-2	D-3	D-4	D-5	D-6	D-7	D-8	D-9	D-11	D-22
1	5 pt	6 pt	6 pt	6 pt	6 pt	6 pt	8 pt	2 pt	4 pt	6 pt	6 pt
2	6 pt	5 pt	6 pt	8 pt	6 pt	8 pt	6 pt	8 pt	6 pt	5 pt	10 pt
3	6 pt	6 pt	5 pt	2 pt	8 pt	8 pt	4 pt	10 pt	8 pt	6 pt	4 pt
4	6 pt	8 pt	2 pt	5 pt	2 pt	8 pt	8 pt	2 pt	2 pt	10 pt	5 pt
5	6 pt	6 pt	8 pt	2 pt	5 pt	6 pt	6 pt	8 pt	8 pt	6 pt	4 pt
6	6 pt	8 pt	8 pt	8 pt	6 pt	5 pt	4 pt	8 pt	8 pt	6 pt	6 pt
7	8 pt	6 pt	4 pt	8 pt	6 pt	4 pt	5 pt	6 pt	6 pt	10 pt	10 pt
8	2 pt	8 pt	10 pt	2 pt	8 pt	8 pt	6 pt	5 pt	6 pt	10 pt	2 pt
9	4 pt	6 pt	8pt	2 pt	8 pt	8 pt	6 pt	6 pt	5 pt	8 pt	4 pt
11	6 pt	5 pt	6 pt	10 pt	6 pt	6 pt	10 pt	10 pt	8 pt	5 pt	8 pt
22	6 pt	10 pt	4 pt	5 pt	4 pt	6 pt	10 pt	2 pt	4 pt	8 pt	5 pt

POINT RATINGS

10 POINTS = EXCELLENT

8 POINTS   = VERY GOOD

6 POINTS   = GOOD

5 POINTS   = STRONG AFFINITY/MODERATE

4 POINTS   = BELOW AVERAGE

2 POINTS   = POOR

Go to page 168, "Compatibility Score Charts" for instructions for determining compatibility using Chart I.

CHART II

ALL THE OTHER NUMBERS COMPATIBILITY CHART
(THE PERSONALITY, ATTITUDE, CHARACTER, SOUL URGE, AND HIDDEN AGENDA)

PERSON #2	PERSON #1 1	2	3	4	5	6	7	8	9	11	22
1	5 pt	6 pt	4 pt	6 pt	10 pt	6 pt	8 pt	2 pt	4 pt	6 pt	6 pt
2	6 pt	5 pt	4 pt	8 pt	8 pt	10 pt	6 pt	6 pt	6 pt	5 pt	8 pt
3	4 pt	4 pt	5 pt	2 pt	10 pt	8 pt	2 pt	10 pt	8 pt	4 pt	2 pt
4	6 pt	8 pt	2 pt	5 pt	2 pt	10 pt	8 pt	2 pt	2 pt	8 pt	5 pt
5	10 pt	8 pt	10 pt	2 pt	5 pt	4 pt	6 pt	8 pt	10 pt	8 pt	4 pt
6	6 pt	10 pt	8 pt	10 pt	4 pt	5 pt	4 pt	6 pt	8 pt	10 pt	8 pt
7	8 pt	6 pt	2 pt	8 pt	6 pt	4 pt	5 pt	4 pt	6 pt	10 pt	8 pt
8	2 pt	6 pt	10 pt	2 pt	8 pt	6 pt	4 pt	5 pt	6 pt	8 pt	2 pt
9	4 pt	6 pt	8 pt	2 pt	10 pt	8 pt	6 pt	6 pt	5 pt	8 pt	2 pt
11	6 pt	5 pt	4 pt	8 pt	8 pt	10 pt	10 pt	8 pt	8 pt	5 pt	8 pt
22	6 pt	8 pt	2 pt	5 pt	4 pt	8 pt	8 pt	2 pt	2 pt	8 pt	5 pt

POINT RATINGS

10 POINTS = EXCELLENT

8 POINTS = VERY GOOD

6 POINTS = GOOD

5 POINTS = STRONG AFFINITY/MODERATE

4 POINTS = BELOW AVERAGE

2 POINTS = POOR

Go to page 169, "Compatibility Score Charts" for instructions for determining compatibility using Chart I.

COMPATIBILITY SCORE CHARTS

Use the following steps to complete DESTINY COMPATIBILITY SCORE CHART below:

(1) Enter the initials of each person being analyzed for Destiny compatibility in box (Each row represents a different couple).

(2) Find Person #1's Destiny number in the top row of the Chart I - Destiny Number Compatibility and follow it down the chart to the Destiny number of Person #2. In box B below, enter the points in the square associated with that combination.

(3) Use Chart I again to compare Person #1's Destiny number to Person #2's Personality and enter the points in box C, below.

(4) Do the same as in (3) above for box D, comparing Person #1's Destiny number to Person #2's Character number.

(5) Finally, enter the total points from B, C, and D in box E.

#1 Numbers: Destiny   _____
#2 Numbers: Destiny   _____
                   Personality   _____
                   Character   _____

DESTINY NUMBER COMPATIBILITY
SCORE CHART

#1 and #2 Initials	1 Destiny + 2 Destiny	1 Destiny + 2 Personality	1 Destiny + 2 Character	Total Points
A	B	C	D	E

EXAMPLE:

PRESIDENT BILL CLINTON - Destiny No. 11.

FIRST LADY HILLARY CLINTON—Destiny No. 3; Personality No. 8;
Character No. 6

#1 and #2 Initials	1 Destiny + 2 Destiny	1 Destiny + 2 Personality	1 Destiny + 2 Character	Total Points
A	B	C	D	E
BC/HC	6 pts	10 pts	6 pts	22 pts

CHART II—ALL THE OTHER NUMBERS

Use the following steps to complete the PERSONALITY, ATTITUDE,
CHARACTER, SOUL URGE, and HIDDEN AGENDA COMPATIBIL-
ITY SCORE CHART below:

(1) Enter the initials of both people being analyzed in box A. (Each row represents a different couple.)

(2) For boxes B, C, D, E, and F, use Chart II—All Other Numbers (exclusively) to determine the compatibility ratings.

(3) In box B, enter the points which result from comparing Person #1's Personality number to Person #2's Personality number.

(4) In box C, enter the points resulting from comparing the Attitude numbers of Persons #1 and #2.

(5) Do the same for the Character numbers, and enter the points in box D.

(6) Do the same for both Soul Urge numbers, and enter the points in box E.

(7) Compare both Hidden Agenda number, and enter the points in box F.

(8) Add all the points in boxes B, C. D, E, and F, and enter the total in box G.

#1 Numbers: #2 Numbers:

Personality   ____   Personality   ____

Attitude   ____   Attitude   ____

Character   ____   Character   ____

Soul Urge   ____   Soul Urge   ____

Hidden Agenda   ____   Hidden Agenda   ____

ALL OTHER NUMBERS COMPATIBILITY SCORE CHART

Initials	Personality	Attitude	Character	Soul Urge	Hidden Agenda	Total
A	B	C	D	E	F	G

Score from Destiny Number Compatibility Score Chart Box E: _____

Score from All Other Numbers Compatibility Score Chart Box G: _____

TOTAL COMPATIBILITY SCORE RATING: _____

EXAMPLES:

PRESIDENT BILL CLINTON: Personality No. 1; Attitude No. 9; Character No. 6; Soul Urge No. 11; Hidden Agenda No. 4

FIRST LADY HILLARY CLINTON: Personality No. 8; Attitude No. 1; Character No. 6; Soul Urge No. 3; Hidden Agenda No. 3

Initials A	Personality B	Attitude C	Character D	Soul Urge E	Hidden Agenda F	Total G
BC/HC	2 pts.	4 pts.	5 pts.	4 pts.	2 pts.	17 pts.

To determine the total Point Rating of Bill and Hillary, add together the their score of 22 from Chart I to the 17 points from Chart II. Total Score for Bill and Hillary is 39. See Point Ratings on page 172.

POINT RATINGS

TOTAL POINTS	**RATING**	
60-80	Excellent	This means you like to do many of the same things; you may have similar tastes; you enjoy the same types of people as friends, and, in some cases have the same kinds of goals and aspirations. This is the best of the best, so be happy!
47-59	Very Good	You're lucky in love and friendship with this relationship! It indicates you will have much in common and feel a strong attraction to one another. Lucky you!
34-46	Good	You've got a good thing going with this relationship. Although you may have an occasional kink to work out, this score indicates that you have an above average relationship! It's not the best, but at least it's pretty good!
21-33	Below Average	This relationship can work, but it will take effort. You might want to determine the reasons why you stay in this relationship. Your answer may be enlightening.
8-20	Poor	Oops! If this is an ongoing relationship, it must be a connection related to negative pastlife karma because otherwise it is doubtful that you would be together or that you would have taken the time to

determine its compatibility rating. This one would need a lot of work to make it work!

4 or more of the same number	Strong Affinity	If you have 4 or more of the same numbers, you have a Strong Affinity relationship. These relationships can be either good or not so good depending on whether one of the pair wants to control the other. That scenario is most likely to occur when the Strong Affinity numbers are 1s and 8s. Also, as the old adage goes, "with familiarity grows contempt," you may have too much in common and grow totally bored with one another over time. Or, on the positive side, it can be the most compatible relationship of your life when both parties respect and admire each other's strengths and opinions.

Chapter 11
Questions People Ask

THE MOST FREQUENTLY ASKED QUESTION IS, "WHAT IS MY NUMBER?"

As stated in Chapter 1, there are six primary numbers in your numerological chart that affect your character and attitude. There's the Personality number, the Destiny number, the Character, Soul Urge, and the Hidden Agenda, each of which has a significant feature for defining and explaining how unique you are.

IS THERE ONE SPECIAL NUMBER THAT IS MORE "YOU" THAN ANY OTHER?

Well, yes and no. Numerologists agree that there is, in fact, such a number, but they don't all agree on which number it is. Some say it's the Destiny number—the full addition of your birth date. Others say it's the Character number—the full addition of your name.

After giving thousands of readings and performing at parties using the birth date exclusively to describe a person, I have always favored the Destiny number first, which is derived from the full addition of your birth date; and next, the Personality number, derived from the day of the month you were born. Even though your name from birth lays down the blueprint of your life, and you retain the vibrational qualities of the numbers derived from it throughout your life (even if you *never* use it), when you change your name, the longer you go by the new name, the greater effect its vibration will have on you. Therefore, in my opinion, the name numbers are not as potent as the numbers from the birth date.

The Destiny number indicates the basic path you will take in your life, the types of people you will be most attracted to, and your fundamental environment needs and desires. This aspect of your character may not become apparent to you until you begin your own independent journey (away from your parents' home), when the true personality of your spirit begins to solidify. If you aren't at that point yet, understanding the Destiny number now can give you a head start for understanding why you are motivated to do what you do and choose the relationships with others that you do.

WHAT NUMBER BRINGS ME LUCK?

Many people have numbers they feel are mysteriously connected to them. If you have seen a pattern of a particular number showing up in your life—or if you simply have a strong feeling about some number—you've probably connected with your inner voice that knows what is best for you. Do not negate a "feeling" or a "sense" about a number, because whether it affects you in a positive or negative way, it is always best to follow you intuition.

Try this exercise: Add together the numbers of all the addresses where you have resided and reduce the compound to a single digit. For example, if you lived at 3257 Main Street, the number in that address would reduce to a single digit as follows: $3+2+5+7 = 17$, and $1+7 = 8$. That house would be considered an 8 house. The 0 in an address is always zero, and therefore you simply cancel it out of the numbers you are adding.

Then, take the numbers in your Social Security number and reduce them to a single digit in the same way. Do the same for other numbers: Your driver's license number, your telephone number(s), and any other numbers that figure prominently in your life. You might also figure the single-digit number of significant dates in your life, such as the day you married, the day you divorced (some people consider divorce fortunate!), the day you signed the papers on your first house, or perhaps the days of the month your children were born.

When you've done all that, is there one particular number that crops up again and again? If so, it could be your lucky number.

If not, your lucky number can be either the day of the month you were born (your Personality number) or the full addition of your birth date (your Destiny number). It's not unusual to find that one of those numbers is the same as an often-occurring number in your life. Personally, I use my

Destiny number as my first choice "lucky number," and my Personality number as my second choice.

Once you know your lucky number, or think you do, test it. For example, if you go to the horse races, and you were born on November 25, 1954, you might have special luck if you were to attend the races on the 1st or the 25th of the month. (The number 1 is the Destiny number for that birth date). When your Personality number is 25, and 2+5 = 7, you might have luck on the other 7 days of the month, too, like the 7th or the 16th. Or you might try going on the other 1 days (the 1 being your Destiny vibration), like the 10th, 19th, and 28th (2 + 8 = 10, 1 + 0 = 1).

My Destiny number is the 22, and when I have gone to the horse races (something I do not do with any frequency), I have gone exclusively on the 22nd day of a month. The other power numbers in my life are 3, 4, 5, and 6. I, therefore, have only bet on races 3, 4, 5, and 6 and on the jockeys or horses that ride under those numbers. Although horse racing is not a hobby, but more like an occasional pastime, when I have strictly stuck to the above numerological formula, I have consistently won more than I spent (including the parking, seats, etc.).

WHAT NUMBERS ARE COMPATIBLE WITH MINE?

See Chapter 9 on Relationships and Compatibility.

WILL I BE FAMOUS?

Anyone can become famous, no matter what their numbers may be. I study biographies of famous people and have one set of books that offers me short bios and the full birth dates of sixty famous and infamous people on every day of the year. Those books have given me the understanding that anyone who maintains a focus and sets a goal to be famous, can be. The mind is our most powerful tool, and regardless of what the letters of your name and the numbers of your birth date reduce to, you have the potential to be great at something! The trick is being cognizant of the things that spark the greatest interest in you, or the greatest desire to learn more, because it is then that you are tapping into your "fame" calling. Fame doesn't always mean that you will be revered by the masses or have your name in lights over a marquee. It can mean that your name becomes very well known in your field of endeavor, among your peers and colleagues, such as being a scientist or an anthropologist, or even a skateboard designer.

WILL I HAVE MONEY IN MY LIFE?

This simple question can be answered only in a complex way. Your numbers tell you why you might want money, what you're likely to do with it, sometimes when you will get it and how long you might keep it, and what your general attitude is regarding it—but no set of numbers can make you rich. It is up to you to manifest that reality. Most people have money in differing amounts, but may spend it quickly, or lack prudence with it—thus effecting a money roller coaster in their lives.

Your Personality and Destiny numbers are the most reflective of how you will handle money. How these two numbers work together is important, too.

For example, if you have a 1 Personality number, you would be more inclined to be a risk taker. If you also have a 4 Destiny number, you are likely to ensure that you have a solid and secure nest egg before you take such risks with your money. With this number combination, you will still be inclined to invest in speculative ventures because the 1 likes to pioneer and trailblaze, but the 4 Destiny number will have a more logical and grounding effect on your purchases.

Another example: If you have an 8 Destiny, you have a very calculating mind that helps you to acquire money. Almost everyone who has an 8 Destiny enjoys getting a "deal" for their money. If your have a 6 Personality number to go with that 8, you will be quite prudent and wise with your spending, especially inclined toward quality purchases, as opposed to quantity.

Generally speaking, the numbers and their bearing on money matters are as follows:

1 Personality	speculative, risk-taking, enjoys a good financial adventure!
1 Destiny	needs to feel in control, so will speculate when funds are ample enough to do so, or not at all. Must feel knowledgeable and have a secure understanding of whatever financial manipulation process he/she employs.
2 Personality	is usually a spendthrift because of their love of luxury, comfort, and giving to others.
2 Destiny	purchases quality and comfort—may overspend when purchasing beautiful things, clothing, literature, music, and physical pleasures.
3 Personality	happy-go-lucky personality, spends freely when money is available.
3 Destiny	has a "luck" factor. Money comes in when needed. Likes to spend money on fine threads, living environment, and can spend lavishly for entertaining and entertainment.
4 Personality	practical and conscientious about spending, but enjoys sharing his/her bounty with friends. Usually budgets and has an impressive savings account.
4 Destiny	risk-taking with career but not with money. Doesn't like to gamble, but may take a chance with savings to start own business.
5 Personality	is risk-taking, impulsive, a spendthrift. Loves to buy everything!
5 Destiny	risk-taking, impulsive, a spendthrift. Has hard time saving.
6 Personality	is conscientious and practical. Likes to research and analyze products before purchasing. Likes to buy quality.
6 Destiny	a soft-touch for helping friends in need with money and other things. May overspend at times, but works diligently to bring in enough to cover all expenses.

7 Personality	unique approach to money. Some 7s constantly want more while other 7s feel money falls out of the heavens into their laps.
7 Destiny	not likely to overspend or underspend. Moderate unless involved in something risqué (which is not unlikely).
8 Personality	penny-pinching at times and a spendthrift at others.
8 Destiny	likes a "deal" and calculates to get it. Desires money and all the fine things it can buy—and usually works hard to get it.
9 Personality	wants the finest and won't settle for less. It doesn't matter what the income, this number will always buy the best, the most expensive.
9 Destiny	wants, desires, needs the best! Can't live happily without the best clothes, car, home, neighborhood, etc. Will work to get it, but many desire and plan to marry into money.
11 Personality	likes the finest, but will make due with whatever your money will allow. Will always have an expensive look whether or not you spend the money to get it.
11 Destiny	comparable to the 11 Personality number. Likes to entertain and will spend freely to do so.
22 Personality	can overspend when the funds are available and then suffers the consequences by not spending for a long period of time.
22 Destiny	can be a spendthrift or somewhat stingy. Is a maverick and doesn't like the rules that go with checks and balances. Tends to be in debt.

HOW LONG WILL I LIVE?

There are some people—mostly men—who want to know this. Numbers rarely provide a specific answer to this question, and even if they did, I prefer not to answer it. It is my opinion that this is not a question that should even be asked. What if you were told you will live to be 75.

Regardless of whether you want to believe that or not, you would probably store that information away in your head and perhaps subconsciously set yourself up for believing you would die at age 75. That is the best reason I know why most professional metaphysical readers do not give an answer to that question.

Some other popular questions require more advanced numerology than is presented in this book. These include: When will I be married? How many children will I have? Will I have more than one marriage? Is my husband faithful?, etc. The answers to these questions can be found most expediently by logging onto my website to set up a personal reading, or consulting another reliable, dedicated, and experienced numerologist.

For those who would like:

- A personalized numerology reading
- Sally Faubion's e-mail address,
- Personalized birthday greeting cards based on numerology,
- Colored print-out of your Wizard's Star,
- Further information about the author,
- Ordering the book

Contact **www.motivationalnumerology.com** or **www.sfnumber.com** or write to Ms. Faubion
at 633 Post Street, #282,
San Francisco, CA 94109

Chapter 12
Famous People - Destiny Numbers

The following birth dates are offered to help the student of numerology to analyze birth dates and names of famous people to determine how the numbers apply to their lives. There are some full birth names listed in parentheses. By using the Internet under the Entertainment category, you can find the personal profiles of most famous people (and the internet is a good source for discovering the full names from birth of famous people).

DESTINY NUMBER 1 *(by birth date):*

9/29/1547	Miguel de Cervantes
6/5/1718	Thomas Chippendale
8/15/1769	Napoleon Bonaparte I
5/31/1819	Walt Whitman
2/15/1820	Susan B. Anthony
9/9/1828	Leo Tolstoy
1/25/1874	Somerset Maughan
9/16/1875	J. C. (James Cash) Penny
8/19/1882	Coco Channel
4/16/1889	Charlie Chaplin
7/26/1894	Aldous Huxley
12/14/1894	e.e. Cummings
10/30/1896	Ruth Gordon
7/22/1898	Steven Vincent Benet
7/21/1899	Ernest (Miller) Hemingway
12/16/1899	Noel (Pierce) Coward
4/5/1900	Spencer Tracy
12/5/1901	Walt Disney (Retlow Yensid)
3/2/1904	Dr. Seuss
1/21/1905	Christian Dior
10/28/1907	Edith Head
1/9/1908	Simone de Beauvoir
7/12/1908	Milton Berle (Milton Berlinger)
6/11/1910	Jacques (Yves) Cousteau
8/27/1910	Mother Teresa
3/13/1911	L. Ron Hubbard
12/11/1913	Carlo Ponti
7/12/1917	Andrew Wyeth
11/7/1918	Billy Graham (William Franklin Graham)
2/6/1919	Zsa Zsa Gabor
5/3/1919	Pete Seeger
2/4/1921	Betty Friedan (Naomi Goldstein)
11/22/1921	Rodney Dangerfield (Jacob Cohen)
3/20/1922	Carl Reiner
7/7/1922	Pierre Cardin
11/3/1922	Charles Bronson (Charles Buchinsky)
3/27/1924	Sarah Vaughn
9/30/1924	Truman Capote
8/30/1925	Donald O'Connor
12/8/1925	Sammy Davis, Jr.

3/16/1926	Jerry Lewis
	(Joseph Levitch)
8/29/1926	Ingrid Bergman
10/18/1926	Chuck Berry
3/14/1928	Frank Borman
4/4/1928	Maya Angelou
5/3/1928	James Brown
1/15/1929	Rev. Martin Luther King
	(Michael Luther)
6/27/1930	(Henry) Ross Perot
8/16/1930	Frank Gifford
	(Francis Newton Gifford)
8/25/1930	Sean Connery
	(Thomas Connery)
3/2/1931	Mikhail Gorbachev
3/2/1931	Tom Wolfe
3/11/1931	Rupert Murdock
10/31/1931	Dan Rather
	(Daniel Irvin Rather)
7/6/1932	Della Reese
	(Delloreese Patricia Early)
4/26/1933	Carol Burnett
5/7/1933	Johnny Unitas
11/19/1933	Larry King
	(Lawrence Harvey Zieger)
2/27/1934	Ralph Nader
3/26/1934	Alan Arkin (Roger Short)
9/20/1934	Sophia Loren
	(Sofia Scicolone)
11/9/1934	Carl Sagan
2/17/1935	Jim Brown
	(James Nathaniel Brown)
6/13/1935	Christo (Javacheff)
8/1/1936	Yves St. Laurent
5/12/1937	George (Dennis) Carlin
8/18/1937	Robert Redford
5/1/1939	Judy Collins
4/2/1939	Marvin Gaye
10/14/1939	Ralph Lauren
3/12/1940	Al Jarreau
7/7/1940	Ringo Starr

9/5/1940	Raquel Welch
1/21/1941	Placido Domingo
8/14/1941	David Crosby (Harry Lillis)
11/19/1942	Calvin Klein
	(Richard Klein)
1/19/1943	Janis Joplin
2/9/1943	Joe Pesci
3/8/1943	Lynn Redgrave
7/4/1943	Geraldo Rivera
12/8/1943	Jim Morrison
5/14/1944	George Lucas
11/17/1944	Danny DeVito
11/17/1944	Lauren Hutton
	(Mary Laurence Hutton)
3/6/1945	Rob Reiner
10/16/1946	Suzanne Somers
11/6/1946	Sally (Margaret) Field
12/14/1946	Patty Duke
4/12/1947	David Letterman
10/24/1947	Kevin Klein
2/4/1948	Alice Cooper
	(Vincent Damon Furnier)
3/12/1948	James Taylor
12/3/1948	Ozzy Osbourne
12/12/1948	Samuel L. Jackson
3/2/1949	Eddie Money
5/9/1949	Billy Joel
	(William Martin Joel)
9/23/1949	Bruce Springsteen
10/4/1949	Armand Assante
5/16/1951	Sally Ride
7/5/1951	Huey Lewis
	(Hugh Anthony Cregg III)
9/12/1951	Joe Pantoliano
10/2/1951	Sting
9/2/1952	Jimmy Connors
	(James Scott Connors)
10/1/1952	Vladimir Putin
4/24/1953	Eric Bogosian
	(David Patric Boreanaz)
10/7/1955	Yo Yo Ma

7/9/1956	Tom Hanks	8/29/1971	Carla Gugino
9/16/1956	David Copperfield	3/6/1972	Shaquille O'Neal
4/29/1957	Daniel Day Lewis	8/10/1972	Angie Harmon
4/29/1957	Michelle Pfeiffer	1/16/1973	Josie Davis
12/21/1957	Ray Romano	12/5/1973	Shalom Harlow
3/20/1958	Holly Hunter	4/12/1974	Marley Shelton
11/21/1958	Megan Mullally	6/1/1974	Alanis Morissette
4/27/1959	Sheena Easton	2/22/1975	Drew Barrymore
1/11/1960	Stanley Tucci	6/27/1975	Toby Maguire
2/19/1960	Prince Andrew		(Bobias Vincent Maguire)
9/21/1960	David James Elliott	8/7/1975	Charlize Theron
3/8/1961	Carmyn (Debra) Manheim	10/5/1975	Kate Winslet
6/14/1961	Boy George	12/30/1975	Tiger Woods
9/2/1961	k. d. Lang	12/18/1978	Katie (Noelle) Holmes
	(Kathryn Dawn Lang)	3/7/1980	Laura Prepon
9/29/1961	Tom Sizemore	3/2/1985	Robert Iler
7/3/1962	Tom Cruise		

DESTINY NUMBERS 2 and 11:

	(Thomas Cruise Mapother)	1/27/1756	Wolfgang Amadeus Mozart
8/19/1963	John (Phillip) Stamos	11/11/1744	First Lady Abigail Adams
10/17/1963	Norm Macdonald	1/6/1759	First Lady Martha
2/15/1964	Chris Farley		Todd Washington
5/30/1964	Wynona Judd	5/20/1768	First Lady Dolly Madison
	(Christina Claire Ciminella)	8/17/1786	Davy Crockett
6/10/1965	Elizabeth Hurley	1/31/1797	Franz Schubert
7/9/1965	Jimmy Smits	4/2/1805	Hans Christian Andersen
7/25/1967	Matt LaBlanc	1/19/1809	Edgar Allen Poe
10/4/1967	(Isaac) Live Schreiber	12/5/1830	George Custer
3/28/1968	Lucy Lawless	1/23/1832	Edouard Manet
7/15/1968	Eddie Griffin	2/26/1846	Buffalo Bill Cody
8/14/1968	Catherine Bell	8/15/1860	First Lady Florence Harding
8/14/1968	Halle Berry	7/21/1864	First Lady Frances
9/4/1968	Mike Piazza		Cleveland
5/16/1969	David Boreanaz	5/27/1878	Isadora Duncan
5/25/1969	Anne Heche	1/3/1879	First Lady Grace Coolidge
6/15/1969	Ice Cube (Shea Jackson)	8/12/1881	Cecil B. DeMille
2/17/1971	Denise (Lee) Richards	7/29/1883	Benito Mussolini
3/7/1971	Rachel Weisz	12/6/1883	Kahlil Gibran
4/15/1971	Jason Sehorn	2/21/1887	Anais Nin
6/4/1971	Noah Wyle	7/7/1887	Marc Chagall
6/22/1971	Kurt Warner	10/31/1887	Chiang Kai-shek
7/30/1971	Tom Green		

7/22/1890	Rose Kennedy	9/24/1931	Anthony Newley
2/25/1901	Zeppo Marx	4/11/1932	Debby Reynolds
7/29/1901	Harry Renton Bridges	4/10/1932	Omar Sharif
5/2/1903	Dr. Benjamin Spock	1/20/1934	Arte Johnson
5/29/1903	Bob Hope	8/22/1934	Norman Schwarzkopf
7/17/1904	James Cagney	12/9/1934	Judy Dench
7/26/1905	Gracie Allen	4/16/1935	Bobby Vinton
8/5/1906	John Huston	9/29/1935	Jerry Lee Lewis
9/28/1909	Al Capp	10/1/1935	Julie Andrews
1/7/1911	Butterfly McQueen	6/4/1936	Bruce Dern
2/6/1911	Pres. Ronald Reagan	6/22/1936	Kris Kristofferson
12/14/1911	Spike Jones	4/5/1937	Gen. Colin Powell
1/6/1912	Danny Thomas	3/13/1939	Neil Sedaka
11/5/1912	Roy Rogers	10/23/1940	Pele
12/22/1912	First Lady Bird Johnson	4/28/1941	Ann Margret
2/4/1913	Rosa Parks	2/2/1942	Graham Nash
4/11/1913	Olge Cassini	9/3/1943	Valerie Perrine
1/4/1914	Jane Wyman	11/28/1943	Randy Newman
12/19/1915	Edith Piaf	12/18/1943	Keith Richards
1/29/1916	Victor Mature	3/17/1944	John Sebastian
6/24/1916	John Ciardi	3/26/1944	Diana Ross
12/9/1916	Kirk Douglas	7/31/1944	Geraldine Chaplin
11/27/1917	Buffalo Bob	10/28/1944	Dennis Franz
3/14/1920	Hank Ketchum	3/7/1945	John Heard
7/10/1920	David Brinkley	6/4/1945	Michelle Phillips
6/10/1921	Prince Philip	9/10/1945	Jose Feliciano
7/18/1921	John Glenn	8/19/1946	Pres. Bill Clinton
1/31/1923	Carol Channing	8/28/1946	David Soul
1/31/1923	Norman Mailer	10/26/1946	Pat Sajak
11/30/1923	Efrem Zimbalist, Jr.	1/7/1947	Jann Werner
1/21/1924	Telly Savalas	2/24/1947	Edward J. Olmos
8/3/1926	Tony Bennett	3/14/1947	Billy Chrystal
10/18/1927	George C. Scott	5/3/1947	Doug Henning
1/17/1928	Vidal Sassoon	2/5/1948	Barbara Hershey
3/6/1928	Gabriel Garcia-Marquez	3/22/1948	Andrew Lloyd Webber
4/23/1928	Shirley Temple-Black	3/31/1948	Rhea Perlman
7/28/1929	First Lady Jacqueline	3/31/1948	Al Gore, Jr.
	Kennedy Onassis	6/19/1948	Phylicia Rashad
11/15/1929	Ed Asner	6/28/1948	Kathy Bates
3/22/1930	Stephen Sondheim	7/27/1948	Peggy Fleming
1/5/1931	Robert Duvall	11/14/1948	Prince Charles

12/22/1948	Steve Garvey
12/31/1948	Donna Summer
4/20/1949	Jessica Lange
11/13/1949	Whoopi Goldberg
12/21/1949	Frank Zappa
2/3/1950	Morgan Fairchild
3/20/1950	William Hurt
4/28/1950	Jay Leno
10/31/1950	Jane Pauley
1/12/1951	Kristie Alley
1/30/1951	Charles S. Dutton
7/15/1951	Jesse Ventura
	(James George Janos)
7/24/1951	Lynda Carter
10/30/1951	Harry (Robinson) Hamlin
2/1/1952	Rick James
10/20/1952	Tom Petty
1/10/1953	Pat Benatar
3/8/1953	Jim Rice
8/30/1953	Robert Parish
11/18/1953	Kevin Nealon
12/8/1953	Kim Basinger
12/17/1953	Bill Pullman
9/28/1954	Steve Largent
12/25/1954	Annie Lenox
12/25/1954	Steve Wariner
4/23/1955	Judy Davis
2/3/1956	Nathan (Joseph) Lane
6/11/1956	Joe Montana
1/15/1957	Steve Harvey
3/21/1958	(Leonard) Gary Oldman
8/16/1958	Madonna
9/24/1958	Kevin Sorbo
11/22/1958	Jamie Lee Curtis
1/22/1959	Linda Blair
7/7/1959	Bill Campbell
9/23/1959	Jason Alexander
	(Jay Scott Greenspan)
10/13/1959	Marie Osmond
9/22/1960	Joan Jett
12/1/1960	Carol Alt

12/10/1960	Kenneth Branaugh
12/10/1960	Oliver Platt
4/26/1961	Joan Chen (Chen Chang)
7/23/1961	Woody Harrelson
	(Woodson Tracy)
2/17/1963	Michael Jordan
7/30/1963	Lisa Kudrow
12/16/1963	Benjamin Bratt
2/24/1965	Kristin Davis
4/4/1965	Robert Downey, Jr.
12/23/1965	Eddie Vedder
	(Edward Louis Seversen III)
1/14/1967	Emily Watson
10/5/1967	Guy Pearce
4/19/1968	Ashley Judd
10/22/1968	Shaggy (Orville
	Richard Burrell)
11/12/1968	Sammy Sosa
12/2/1968	Lucy Liu
2/11/1969	Jennifer Aniston
3/1/1969	Javier Bardem
1/29/1970	Heather Graham
7/23/1970	Carisma Carpenter
8/31/1970	Debbie Gibson
10/2/1970	Kelly Ripa
11/19/1970	Peta (Gia) Wilson
4/16/1971	Selena (Selena
	Quintanilla-Perez)
6/5/1971	Mark Wahlberg
8/12/1971	Pete Sampras
9/18/1973	James Marsden
1/16/1974	Kate Moss
9/4/1978	Wes (Cook) Bentley
9/26/1981	Serena Williams
5/5/1981	Danielle (Christine) Fishel
8/28/1982	Lee Ann Rimes

DESTINY NUMBER 3:

9/5/1735	Johann Christian Bach
1/25/1759	Robert Burns
12/16/1776	Jane Austen

2/7/1812	Charles Dickens	11/20/1925	Robert Kennedy
3/14/1804	Johann Strauss	5/25/1926	Miles Davis
11/23/1859	Billy The Kid	4/7/1927	Neil Simon
6/13/1865	William Butler Yeats	6/23/1927	Bob Fosse
2/17/1874	Thomas J. Watson	12/26/1927	Alan King
10/7/1885	Niels Bohr	4/6/1928	James Dewey Watson
2/10/1890	Boris Pasternak	5/23/1928	Rosemary Clooney
12/26/1891	Henry Miller	5/4/1929	Audrey Hepburn
9/24/1896	F. Scott Fitzgerald	6/12/1929	Ann Frank
1/13/1834	Horatio Alger	3/22/1931	William Shatner
7/24/1898	Amelia Earhart	9/25/1931	Barbara Walters
8/13/1899	Alfred Hitchcock	2/22/1932	Sen. Ted Kennedy
4/7/1900	Louis Armstrong	4/11/1932	Joel Grey
10/10/1900	Helen Hayes	4/19/1933	Jayne Mansfield
9/28/1901	William S. Pauly	12/28/1934	Maggie Smith
12/16/1901	Margaret Mead	9/30/1935	Johnny Mathis
5/2/1904	Bing Crosby	10/20/1935	Jerry Orbach
5/11/1904	Salvador Dali	11/1/1935	Gary Player ·
5/26/1907	John Wayne	1/28/1936	Alan Alda
5/23/1910	Scatman Crothers	8/21/1936	Wilt Chamberlain
1/15/1913	Lloyd Bridges	4/6/1937	Merle Haggard
7/18/1913	Red Shelton	4/6/1937	Billy Dee Williams
11/5/1913	Vivien Leigh	7/12/1937	Bill Cosby
4/2/1914	Alec Guiness	7/20/1938	Natalie Wood
12/18/1917	Ossie Davis	7/29/1938	Peter Jennings
4/7/1918	Ann Landers	6/11/1939	Gene Wilder
4/7/1918	Abigail Van Buren	2/23/1940	Peter Fonda
5/15/1918	Eddy Arnold	1/14/1941	Faye Dunaway
10/17/1920	Montgomery Clift	4/20/1941	Ryan O'Neal
5/3/1921	Sugar Ray Robinson	12/12/1941	Dionne Warwick
3/12/1922	Jack Kerouac	9/12/1944	Barry White
6/10/1922	Judy Garland	1/10/1945	Rod Stewart
4/20/1923	Tito Puente	2/9/1945	Mia Farrow
12/3/1923	Maria Callas	10/19/1945	John (Arthur) Lithgow
12/12/1923	Franco Zeffirelli	3/7/1946	Peter Wolf
12/12/1923	Bob Barker	8/20/1946	Connie Chung
7/25/1924	Estelle Getty	12/25/1946	Jimmy Buffet
10/4/1924	Charlton Heston	7/20/1947	Carlos Santana
7/6/1925	Merv Griffin	10/26/1947	Jacklyn Smith
10/3/1925	Gore Vidal	10/26/1947	Sen. Hillary Clinton
11/11/1925	Jonathan Winters	11/25/1947	John Larroquette

1/7/1948	Kenny Loggins		11/25/1965	Dougray (Stephen) Scott
6/2/1948	Jerry Mathers		5/12/1966	Stephen Baldwin
9/26/1948	Olivia Newton John		6/28/1967	Gil Bellows
1/24/1949	John Belushi		7/18/1967	Vin Diesel
5/2/1949	Larry Gatlin		5/10/1968	Erik Palladiro
9/16/1949	Ed Begley, Jr.		7/8/1968	Billy Crudup
12/4/1949	Jeff Bridges		11/13/1968	Steve Zahn
2/22/1950	Julius Erving		12/3/1968	Brendan Fraser
8/25/1950	Ann Archer		11/21/1969	Ken Griffey, Jr.
6/17/1951	Joe Piscopo		3/28/1970	Vince Vaughn
6/7/1952	Liam Neeson		6/16/1970	Chris O'Donnell
12/9/1953	John Malkovich		7/24/1970	Jennifer Lopez
4/7/1954	Tony Dorsett		6/15/1971	Jake Busey (William
4/7/1954	Jackie Chan (Chan			Jacob Busey)
	Kwong-Sang)		9/30/1971	Jenna Elfman
12/26/1954	Ozzie Smith			(Jennifer Mary Butola)
1/18/1955	Kevin Costner		10/20/1971	Snoop Dogg
1/17/1956	David Caruso			(Cordozar Broadus)
7/11/1956	Sela Ward		6/23/1972	Selma Blair
8/9/1957	Melanie Griffith		8/12/1972	Rebecca Gayheart
4/3/1958	Alec Baldwin		8/30/1972	Cameron Diaz
4/21/1958	Tony Danza		10/28/1972	Brad Paisley
4/21/1958	Andie Mac Dowell		11/17/1973	Leslie Bibb
5/29/1958	Annette Benning		3/24/1974	Alyson Harrigan
10/23/1959	Weird Al Yankovic		10/16/1975	Kellie Martin
12/21/1959	Florence Griffith Joyner		3/22/1976	Reese Witherspoon
12/30/1959	Tracy Ullman			(Laura Jean)
11/29/1961	Kim Delaney		8/8/1976	Joshua Scott Chasez (J.C.)
7/23/1962	Eriq LaSalle		2/11/1979	Brandy (Brandy
11/19/1962	Jodi Foster			Rayana Norwood)
11/28/1962	Jon Stewart (Jon		5/15/1981	Jamie-Lynn Sigler
	Stuart Liebowitz)			
10/28/1963	Lauren Holly		**DESTINY NUMBER 4 and 22:**	
6/22/1964	Amy Brenneman		9/4/1530	Ivan The Terrible
7/30/1964	Vivica A. Fox		6/9/1672	Peter The Great
9/19/1964	Trisha Yearwood		4/22/1724	Immanuel Kant
9/28/1964	Janeane Garofalo		7/5/1810	P. T. Barnum
2/7/1965	Chris Rock		12/25/1821	Clara Barton
5/31/1965	Brooke Shields		11/30/1835	Mark Twain
8/28/1965	Shania Twain		4/17/1837	J. P. Morgan
9/27/1965	Steve Kerr		5/6/1856	Sigmund Freud

9/7/1860	Grandma Moses	8/9/1931	Hurricane Jackson
11/7/1867	Marie Curie	10/7/1931	Desmond Tutu
12/31/1869	Henri Matisse	11/6/1931	Mike Nichols
3/26/1874	Robert Frost	4/21/1932	Elaine May
1/6/1878	Carl Sandburg	4/29/1933	Rod McKuen
11/4/1879	Will Rogers	1/22/1934	Bill Bixby
12/21/1879	Joseph Stalin	3/11/1934	Sam Donaldson
9/6/1888	Joseph Kennedy	10/12/1935	Luciano Pavarotti
5/28/1888	Jim Thorpe	12/1/1935	Woody Allen
10/29/1891	Fanny Brice	7/23/1936	Don Drysdale
2/6/1895	Babe Ruth	11/19/1936	Dick Cavett
9/28/1902	Ed Sullivan	5/15/1937	Trini Lopez
4/22/1904	Julius Robert Oppenheimer	11/26/1938	Tina Turner
8/18/1904	Max Factor	2/6/1940	Tom Brokaw
2/3/1907	James A. Michener	1/24/1941	Neil Diamond
12/12/1915	Frank Sinatra	11/5/1941	Art Garfunkel
2/11/1917	Sidney Sheldon	6/18/1942	Paul McCartney
10/21/1917	Dizzy Gillispie	9/24/1942	Linda McCartney
3/9/1918	Micky Spillane	10/23/1942	Michael Crichton
7/14/1918	Ingmar Bergman	2/3/1943	Blythe Danner
4/17/1918	William Holden	10/22/1943	Catherine Deneuve
1/1/1919	J. D. Salinger	3/28/1944	Rick Barry
3/17/1919	Nat King Cole	9/13/1944	Jacqueline Bissett
2/8/1920	Lana Turner	1/29/1945	Tom Selleck
7/21/1920	Isaac Stern	8/31/1945	Itzhak Perlman
8/29/1920	Charlie Parker	1/19/1946	Dolly Parton
9/8/1922	Sid Ceasar	6/14/1946	Donald Trump
6/8/1925	First Lady Barbara Bush	7/13/1946	Cheech Marin
10/13/1925	Lenny Bruce	10/10/1946	Ben Vereen
4/9/1926	Hugh Hefner	3/25/1947	Elton John
5/8/1926	Don Rickles	7/30/1947	Arnold Schwarzenegger
2/10/1927	. Leontyne Price	12/7/1947	Johnny Bench
3/18/1927	George Plimpton	7/28/1949	Vida Blue
7/14/1927	John Chancellor	11/24/1949	Linda Tripp
8/13/1927	Fidel Castro	12/23/1949	Susan Lucci
4/7/1928	James Garner	3/13/1950	William H. Macy
7/22/1928	Orson Bean	4/20/1951	Luther Vandross
9/10/1929	Arnold Palmer	3/2/1952	Laraine Newman
5/4/1930	Roberta Peters	5/18/1952	George Strait
5/31/1930	Clint Eastwood	10/22/1952	Jeff Goldblum
12/6/1930	Dave Brubeck	1/29/1954	Oprah Winfrey

6/15/1954	Jim Belushi
10/2/1954	Lorraine Bracco
3/17/1955	Gary Sinise
7/22/1955	Willem Dafoe (William Dafoe)
10/28/1955	Bill Gates
7/3/1956	Montel Williams
7/30/1956	Delta Burke
7/30/1956	Anita Hill
8/20/1956	Joan Allen
10/18/1956	Martina Navratilova
12/7/1956	Larry Bird
1/26/1957	Eddie Van Halen
2/16/1957	LaVar Burton
4/3/1959	David Hyde Pierce
5/29/1959	Rupert Everett
8/7/1960	David Duchovny
11/12/1961	Nadia Comaneci
11/11/1962	Demi Moore
2/19/1963	Seal (Sealhenry Samuel)
5/25/1963	Mike Myers
6/15/1963	Helen Hunt
9/21/1963	Cecil Fielder
2/18/1964	Matt Dillon
3/17/1964	Rob Lowe
4/7/1964	Russell Crowe
7/22/1964	David Spade
12/8/1964	Terri Hatcher
4/15/1965	Bill Bellamy
9/9/1966	Adam Sandler
1/15/1968	Chad Lowe
1/24/1968	Mary Lou Retton
3/3/1969	Julie Bowen
9/6/1969	Marc Anthony (Marc Antonio Muniz)
11/4/1969	Matthew McConaughey
3/20/1970	Michael Rapaport
5/27/1970	Joseph Finnes
6/26/1970	Sean Hayes
6/26/1970	Chris O'Donnell
1/11/1972	Amanda Peet

11/1/1972	Toni Collette
2/8/1974	Seth Green
7/30/1974	Hilary Swank
9/10/1974	Ryan Phillippe (Matthew Ryan Phillippe)
4/13/1976	Jonathan Brandis
11/15/1976	Virginie Ledoyen
2/21/1979	Jennifer Love Hewitt
4/19/1979	Kate Hudson
10/4/1979	Rachael Leigh Cook
12/19/1980	Marla Sokoloff
4/10/1988	Haley Joel Osment

DESTINY NUMBER 5:

12/25/1642	Isaac Newton
4/13/1743	Pres. Thomas Jefferson
9/1/1804	George Sand
1/4/1809	Louis Braille
2/12/1809	Charles Darwin
2/12/1809	Pres. Abraham Lincoln
1/19/1839	Paul Cezanne
2/25/1841	Pierre Auguste Renoir
3/30/1853	Vincent Van Gogh
1/17/1868	Anton Chekhov
10/3/1873	Emily Post
7/2/1877	Herman Hesse
6/27/1880	Helen Keller
1/30/1882	Pres. Franklin Roosevelt
2/2/1882	James Joyce
11/15/1887	Georgia O'Keefe
5/11/1888	Irving Berlin
10/8/1895	Juan Peron
9/25/1897	William Faulkner
2/1/1901	Clark Gable
2/28/1901	Linus Pauling
5/7/1901	Gary Cooper
12/27/1901	Marlene Dietrich
2/27/1902	John Steinbeck
4/14/1904	Sir John Gielgud
1/15/1906	Aristotle Onassis
7/27/1906	Lou Dorocher

1/3/1909	Victor Borge	10/23/1934	Chi Chi Rodriguez
6/7/1909	Jessica Tandy	4/19/1935	Dudley Moore
3/26/1911	Tennessee Williams	2/11/1936	Burt Reynolds
6/5/1911	Rosalind Russell	5/17/1936	Dennis Hopper
11/7/1913	Albert Camus	6/15/1937	Waylon Jennings
4/21/1915	Anthony Quinn	1/10/1938	Willie McCovey
6/10/1915	Saul Bellow	4/7/1938	Jerry Brown
5/1/1916	Glenn Ford	8/21/1938	Kenny Rogers
11/4/1916	Walter Cronkite	7/30/1939	Peter Bogdanovich
3/2/1917	Desi Arnaz, Sr.	9/1/1939	Lily Tomlin
6/17/1917	Dean Martin	10/27/1939	John Cleese
8/6/1917	Robert Mitchum	4/23/1940	Lee Majors
5/7/1919	Evita Peron	10/8/1941	Jesse Jackson
2/18/1920	Jack Palance	4/3/1942	Wayne Newton
8/11/1921	Alex Haley	4/3/1942	Marsha Mason
11/7/1922	Al Hirt	7/18/1942	James Brolin
12/24/1922	Ava Gardner	9/7/1942	Richard Roundtree
1/25/1923	Corazon Aquino	10/15/1942	Penny Marshall
4/3/1924	Marlon Brando	1/14/1943	Holland Taylor
4/3/1924	Doris Day	7/26/1943	Mick Jagger
9/16/1924	Lauren Bacall	11/22/1943	Billy Jean King
10/15/1924	Lee Iacocca	2/21/1944	Tyne Daly (Ellen
5/19/1925	Malcolm X		Tyne Daly)
10/23/1925	Johnny Carson	10/4/1944	Patti LaBelle
11/4/1925	Doris Roberts	1/3/1945	Stephen Stills
6/8/1926	Leroy Neiman	6/25/1945	Carly Simon
9/23/1926	John Coltrane	10/30/1945	Henry Winkler
11/30/1926	Richard Crenna	12/1/1945	Bette Midler
2/20/1927	Sidney Poitier	1/11/1946	Naomi Judd
3/1/1927	Harry Belafonte	4/16/1947	Kareem Abdul-Jabbar
4/27/1927	Coretta Scott King	7/22/1947	Don Henley
8/31/1928	James Coburn	7/12/1948	Richard Simmons
10/20/1928	Dr. Joyce Brothers	8/2/1948	Terry Bradshaw
11/28/1928	Barry Gordy, Jr.	9/19/1948	Jeremy Irons
2/17/1930	Alan Bates	12/25/1948	Barbara Mandrell
1/17/1931	James Earl Jones	12/15/1949	Don Johnson
12/5/1932	Little Richard	2/6/1950	Natalie Cole
4/30/1933	Willie Nelson	4/13/1950	Ron Perlman
6/10/1933	F. Lee Bailey	4/22/1950	Peter Frampton
2/13/1934	George Segal	5/12/1950	Gabriel Bryne
7/17/1934	Donald Sutherland	6/20/1950	Lionel Richie

7/9/1951	Chris Cooper	7/31/1965	J. K. Rowling
9/25/1951	Mark Hamill	10/28/1965	Jarvis Gertz
4/29/1952	Nora Dunn	8/9/1968	Gillian Anderson
5/19/1952	Grace Jones	2/5/1969	Bobby Brown
6/18/1952	Isabella Rossellini	9/25/1969	Catherine Zeta-Jones
12/12/1952	Kathy Rigby	4/29/1970	Andre Agassi
2/21/1953	William Petersen	4/29/1970	Uma Thurman
1/12/1954	Howard Stern	5/10/1970	Gina Philips
2/2/1954	Christie Brinkley	8/25/1970	Claudia Shiffer
3/1/1954	Ron Howard	12/12/1970	Jennifer Connolly
3/28/1954	Reba McIntire	1/31/1971	Minnie Driver
4/9/1954	Dennis Quaid		(Amelia Driver)
12/28/1954	Denzel Washington	12/19/1972	Alyssa Milano
8/4/1955	Billy Bob Thornton	7/23/1973	Omar (Haskin) Epps
12/18/1955	Ray Liotta	11/19/1973	Savion Glover
1/10/1956	Shawn Colvin	10/28/1974	Joaquin Phoenix
8/21/1956	Kim Cattrall	6/4/1975	Angelina Jolie Voight
1/26/1958	Anita Baker	11/8/1975	Tara Reid
1/26/1958	Ellen DeGeneres	6/10/1978	Shane West
	(Judith Olivia DeGeneres)	2/13/1979	Mena Suvari
2/16/1958	Ice T (Tracy Morrow)	2/12/1980	Christina Ricci
8/28/1958	Scott Hamilton	6/17/1980	Venus Williams
11/16/1958	Marg Helgenberger	3/28/1981	Julia Stiles
	(Mary Helgenberger)		
1/16/1959	Sade	**DESTINY NUMBER 6:**	
8/17/1960	Sean Penn	4/5/1725	Giovanni Casanova
8/26/1960	Branford Marsalis	3/6/1806	Elizabeth Barrett Browning
2/4/1961	Dennis Savard	2/11/1847	Thomas Edison
6/9/1961	Michael J. Fox	12/28/1856	Pres. Woodrow Wilson
12/30/1961	Ben Johnson	10/14/1890	Pres. Dwight Eisenhower
3/2/1962	Jon Bon Jovi	9/15/1890	Agatha Christie
	(John Bongiovi)	11/22/1890	Charles DeGaulle
8/6/1962	Michelle Yeoh	1/3/1892	J.R.R. Tolkien
11/30/1962	Bo Jackson	5/10/1899	Fred Astaire
12/2/1962	Tracy Austin	9/18/1905	Greta Garbo
4/18/1963	Conan O'Brien	1/18/1904	Cary Grant
12/19/1963	Jennifer Beals	4/2/1908	Buddy Ebsen
3/9/1964	Juliette Binoche	5/28/1908	Ian (Lancaster) Fleming
6/15/1964	Courtney Cox Arquette	3/1/1910	David Niven
2/9/1965	Julie Warner	1/18/1913	Danny Kaye
4/16/1965	Martin Lawrence	3/29/1918	Pearl Bailey

5/9/1918	Mike Wallace	3/31/1943	Christopher Walken
3/1/1919	Harry Carey	8/17/1943	Robert DeNiro
1/20/1920	Fredrico Fellini	11/5/1943	Sam Shepard
4/16/1921	Peter Ustinov	2/13/1944	Stockard Channing
11/26/1922	Charles Shulz	5/28/1944	Gladys Knight
3/6/1923	Ed McMahon	11/12/1945	Neil Young
9/16/1925	B. B. King	11/21/1945	Goldie Hawn
2/21/1927	Erma Bombeck	2/20/1946	Brenda Blethyn
11/30/1927	Robert Guillaume		(Brenda Ann Bottle)
1/11/1929	Rod Taylor	7/6/1946	Sylvester Stallone
5/25/1929	Beverly Sills	7/15/1946	Linda Ronstadt
8/20/1931	Don King	8/5/1946	Loni Anderson
7/2/1932	Wendy's Dave Thomas	12/28/1946	Herbie Green
3/14/1933	Michael Caine	9/21/1947	Stephen King
3/14/1933	Quincy Jones	10/29/1947	Richard Dreyfuss
5/3/1933	James Brown	12/18/1947	Steven Spielberg
8/18/1933	Roman Polanski	3/26/1948	Steve Tyler
2/5/1934	Hank Aaron	4/7/1948	John Oates
3/4/1934	Jane Goodall	6/23/1948	Clarence Thomas
3/31/1934	Shirley Jones	3/16/1949	Erik Estrada
7/17/1935	Dianna Carroll	6/22/1949	Meryl Streep
12/21/1935	Phil Donahue	11/8/1949	Bonnie Raitt
12/30/1935	Sandy Koufax	12/25/1949	Sissy Spacek
5/9/1936	Albert Finney	5/13/1950	Stevie Wonder
4/10/1936	John Madden	5/13/1950	Peter Gabriel
12/29/1936	Mary Tyler Moore	2/15/1951	Jane Seymour
1/30/1937	Vanessa Redgrave	10/7/1951	Julie Kavner
2/2/1937	Tommy Smothers	9/25/1952	Christopher Reeve
4/27/1937	Sandy Dennis	7/25/1954	Walter Payton
2/1/1938	Sherman Hemsley	11/3/1954	Adam Ant
4/26/1938	Duane Eddy	12/11/1954	Jermaine Jackson
11/19/1938	Ted Turner	3/19/1955	Bruce Willis
4/7/1939	David Frost	5/17/1955	Bill Paxton
4/7/1939	Francis Ford Coppola	6/6/1956	Bjorn Borg
8/12/1939	George Hamilton	3/26/1957	Leeza Gibbons
11/18/1939	Margaret Atwood	5/23/1958	Drew Carey
2/8/1940	Nick Nolte	8/29/1958	Michael Jackson
2/8/1940	Ted Koppel	10/27/1958	Simon Lebon
10/9/1940	John Lennon	3/6/1959	Tom Arnold
3/15/1941	Mike Love	8/10/1959	Rosanne Arquette
10/25/1942	Helen Reddy	9/27/1959	Shaun Cassidy

4/3/1961	Eddie Murphy	3/21/1685	Johann Bach
9/25/1961	Heather Locklear	12/16/1770	Ludwig van Beethoven
3/3/1962	Jackie Joyner-Kersee	2/22/1810	Frederic Chopin
3/3/1962	Herschel Walker	10/22/1811	Franz Liszt
3/12/1962	Darryl Strawberry	11/22/1819	George Eliot
3/21/1962	Rosie O'Donnell	12/10/1830	Emily Dickinson
3/21/1962	Matthew Broderick	5/7/1840	Peter Tchaikovsky
6/17/1963	Greg Kinnear	1/7/1844	St. Bernadette of Lourdes
10/22/1963	Brian Boitano	6/7/1848	Paul Gauguin
3/10/1964	Prince Edward	4/18/1857	Clarence Darrow
5/8/1964	Melissa Gilbert	2/3/1874	Gertrude Stein
9/22/1964	Bonnie Hunt	11/30/1874	Winston Churchill
11/11/64	Clarista Flockhart	7/3/1878	George M. Cohan
11/29/1964	Don Cheadle	12/8/1886	Diego Rivera
9/3/1965	Charlie Sheen	4/2/1891	Max Ernst
9/2/1966	Salma Hayek	10/30/1893	Charles Atlas
12/8/1966	Sinead O'Connor	5/21/1898	Armand Hammer
10/26/1968	Tim Cavanagh	9/26/1898	George Gershwin
8/18/1969	Edward Norton , Jr.	9/24/1900	Stephen Bechtel
8/18/1969	Christian Slater	2/20/1902	Ansel Adams
10/6/1970	Amy Jo Johnson	10/1/1904	Vladmir Horowitz
8/15/1972	Ben Affleck	6/3/1906	Josephine Baker
12/29/1972	Jude Law	5/20/1908	Jimmy Stewart
6/16/1973	Eddie Cibrian	7/14/1912	Woody Guthrie
10/3/1973	Neve Campbell	10/27/1914	Dylan Thomas
8/12/1975	Casey Affleck	5/29/1917	Pres. John F. Kennedy
4/14/1977	Sarah Michele Gellar	5/1/1918	Jack Parr
5/12/1978	Jason Biggs	8/25/1918	Leonard Bernstein
6/11/1978	Joshua Jackson	5/18/1919	Margot Fonteyn
12/23/1978	Estella Warren	7/24/1920	Bella Abzug
4/12/1979	Claire Danes	2/18/1922	Helen Gurley Brown
1/31/1981	Justin Randall Timberlake	4/22/1925	Aaron Spelling
4/28/1981	Jessica Alba	5/12/1925	Yogi Berra
12/2/1981	Britney Spears	11/24/1925	William F. Buckley
7/24/1982	Anna Paquin	4/21/1926	Queen Elizabeth II
11/29/1982	Lucas Black	6/1/1926	Marilyn Monroe
		6/28/1926	Mel Brooks

DESTINY NUMBER 7:

		5/9/1928	Pancho Gonzalez
9/20/356 BC	Alexander The Great	1/20/1930	Buzz Aldrin
4/23/1564	William Shakespeare	8/4/1930	Neil Armstrong
7/15/1605	Rembrandt van Rijn	5/6/1931	Willie Mays

2/26/1932	Johnny Cash	8/27/1952	Paul Reubens
12/7/1932	Ellen Burstyn	8/25/1954	Elvis Costello
8/1/1933	Dom DeLuise	4/29/1954	Jerry Seinfeld
9/18/1933	Robert Blake	12/21/1954	Chris Evert Lloyd
1/16/1934	Marilyn Horne	2/21/1955	Kelsey Grammer
6/11/1934	Gene Wilder	5/18/1955	Chow Yun-Fat
3/31/1935	Herb Alpert	11/30/1955	Billy Idol
3/31/1935	Richard Chamberlain	12/20/1955	Michael Badalucco
4/21/1935	Charles Grodin	1/3/1956	Mel Gibson
9/24/1936	Jim Henson	11/20/1956	Bo Derek
9/6/1936	Buddy Holly	7/23/1957	Philip Seymore Hoffman
6/16/1938	Joyce Carol Oates	11/19/1957	Allison Jonney
8/3/1940	Martin Sheen	12/9/1957	Donny Osmond
9/11/1940	Brian DePalma	8/2/1959	Victoria Jackson
11/27/1940	Bruce Lee	4/23/1960	Valerie Bertinelli
1/9/1941	Joan Baez	8/10/1960	Antonio Banderas
6/22/1941	Ed Bradley	9/9/1960	Hugh Grant
7/30/1941	Paul Anka	5/12/1961	Ving Rhames
12/16/1941	Leslie Stahl		(Irving Rhames)
8/1/1942	Gerry Garcia	7/1/1961	Carl Lewis
1/17/1942	Mohammed Ali	7/1/1961	Princess Diana
7/10/1943	Arthur Ashe	12/22/1962	Ralph Finnes
7/28/1943	Bill Bradley	1/14/1963	Steven Soderbergh
5/2/1944	Joe Cocker	6/9/1963	Johnny Depp
9/25/1944	Michael Douglas	4/8/1966	Robin (Virginia)
3/3/1945	Eric Clapton		Wright Penn
3/12/1946	Liza Minnelli	5/24/1967	Eric Close
5/9/1946	Candace Bergen	8/21/1967	Carrie-Anne Moss
5/18/1946	Reggie Jackson	2/8/1968	Gary Coleman
6/17/1946	Barry Manilow	8/19/1969	Matthew Perry
10/4/1946	Susan Sarandon	4/13/1970	Ricky Schroder
12/20/1946	Uri Geller	7/10/1970	Henry Simmons
12/20/1946	John Spencer	10/25/1970	Adam Goldberg
2/2/1947	Farrah Fawcett	11/6/1970	Ethan Hawke
3/19/1947	Glenn Close	3/13/1971	Annabeth Gish
2/28/1948	Bernadette Peters		(Ann Elizabeth Gish)
10/9/1950	Jackson Browne	4/12/1971	Nicholas Brendon
9/9/1951	Michael Keaton	4/12/1971	Shannen Doherty
6/20/1952	John Goodman	10/6/1971	Jeremy Sisto
7/1/1952	Dan Aykroyd	1/31/1973	Portia de Rossi
8/18/1952	Patrick Swayze		(Amanda Rogers)

10/31/1973	Chris Tucker		10/27/1924	Ruby Dee
1/30/1974	Christian Bale		1/26/1925	Paul Newman
8/23/1974	Ray Park		4/14/1925	Rod Steiger
11/11/1974	Leonardo DiCaprio		6/21/1925	Maureen Stapleton
1/29/1975	Sara Gilbert		9/9/1925	Cliff Robertson
5/25/1975	Lauryn Hill		12/23/1926	Robert Bly
8/2/1977	Edward Furlong		9/16/1927	Peter Falk
8/26/1980	Macaulay Culkin		1/5/1928	Walter Mondale
6/9/1981	Natalie Portman		3/12/1928	Edward Albee
3/11/1982	Thora Birch		4/11/1928	Ethel Kennedy
			12/30/1928	Bo Diddley

DESTINY NUMBER 8:

			4/1/1929	Jane Powell
3/21/1685	Johann S. Bach		9/5/1929	Bob Newhart
1/4/1785	Jacob Grimm		10/31/1929	Lee Grant
1/7/1800	Pres. Millard Fillmore		11/30/1929	Dick Clark
10/16/1854	Oscar Wilde		9/21/1931	Larry Hagman
12/30/1865	Rudyard Kipling		9/30/1931	Angie Dickinson
10/30/1885	Ezra Pound		10/20/1931	Mickey Mantle
1/26/1880	Gen. Douglas MacArthur		12/11/1931	Rita Moreno
6/25/1903	George Orwell		4/15/1933	Roy Clark
5/22/1907	Laurence Olivier		4/15/1933	Elizabeth Mongtomery
1/16/1908	Ethel Merman		4/5/1934	Frank Gorshin
3/23/1908	Joan Crawford		9/17/1935	Ken Kesey
4/22/1908	Eddy Albert		12/14/1935	Lee Remick
8/27/1908	Pres. Lyndon B. Johnson		9/25/1936	Juliette Prowse
8/23/1912	Gene Kelly		12/21/1937	Jane Fonda
7/14/1913	Pres. Gerald Ford		2/21/1938	Judy Blume
10/28/1914	Jonas Salk		4/10/1938	Don Meredith
12/26/1914	Richard Widmark		12/29/1938	Jon Voight
1/9/1915	Fernando Lamas		10/30/1939	Grace Slick
5/5/1915	Alice Faye		2/19/1940	Smokey Robinson
8/29/1915	Ingrid Bergman		3/9/1940	Raul Julia
4/5/1916	Gregory Peck		8/22/1940	Valerie Harper
5/21/1917	Raymond Burr		5/24/1941	Bob Dylan
10/7/1917	June Allyson		8/3/1941	Martha Stewart
1/14/1919	Andy Rooney		8/30/1941	Elizabeth Ashley
1/24/1918	Oral Roberts		4/24/1942	Barbra Streisand
10/22/1920	Timothy Leary		5/5/1942	Tammy Wynette
5/7/1922	Darren McGavin		11/17/1942	Martin Scorsese
3/8/1923	Cyd Charisse		2/25/1943	George Harrison
11/18/1923	Alan Shepard		4/5/1943	Max Gail
6/20/1924	Chet Atkins		5/31/1943	Sharon Gless

11/7/1943	Joni Mitchell	2/19/1967	Denecio Del Toro
8/9/1944	Sam Elliott	1/28/1968	Edward Burns
12/22/1945	Diane Sawyer	2/18/1968	Molly Ringwald
1/5/1946	Diane Keaton	6/14/1968	Yasmine Bleeth
3/12/1946	Liza Minelli	1/18/1969	Jesse L. Martin
8/16/1946	Lesley Ann Warren	7/12/1969	Lisa Nicole Carson
9/15/1946	Tommy Lee Jones	9/10/1969	Johnathon Schaech
9/15/1946	Oliver Stone	3/24/1970	Lara Flynn Boyle
12/30/1946	David Jones	10/8/1970	Matt Damon
4/1/1947	David Eisenhower	9/8/1971	David Arquette
12/29/1947	Ted Danson	4/3/1972	Mili Avital
3/28/1948	Dianne Wiest	5/20/1972	Busta Rhymes
5/26/1948	Stevie Nicks		(Trevor Smith)
8/31/1949	Richard Gere	7/26/1973	Kate Beckinsale
11/28/1949	Paul Shaffer	4/28/1974	Penelope Cruz (Sanchez)
2/18/1950	Cybill Shepherd	1/28/1977	Joseph Anthony Fatone, Jr.
3/26/1950	Teddy Pendergrass		(Joey)
7/12/1951	Cheryl Ladd	3/8/1977	James (William) Van
9/19/1951	Joan Lunden		Der Beek
10/18/1951	Pam Dawber	7/12/1978	Topher Grace
3/4/1954	Catherine O'Hara		(Christopher Grace)
6/19/1954	Kathleen Turner	7/21/1978	Josh Hartnett
4/2/1955	Dana Carvey	5/4/1979	James Lance Bass
12/21/1955	Jane Kaczmanek	7/10/1980	Jessica Simpson
1/21/1957	Geena Davis	3/3/1982	Jessica Biel
12/10/1957	Michael Clarke Duncan	10/11/1985	Michelle Trachtenberg
1/20/1958	Lorenzo Lamas		
1/26/1961	Wayne Gretzky	**DESTINY NUMBER 9:**	
4/14/1961	Robert Carlyle	1/4/1642	Isaac Newton
9/18/1961	James Gandolfini	10/31/1795	John Keats
10/26/1961	Dylan McDermott	7/12/1817	Henry David Thoreau
7/1/1962	Andre Braugher	11/29/1832	Louisa Mae Alcott
10/6/1963	Elisabeth Shue	11/24/1864	Henri de Loulouse-Lautrec
7/26/1964	Sandra Bullock	6/8/1867	Frank Lloyd Wright
8/25/1964	Blair Underwood	10/2/1869	Mahatma Gandhi
8/24/1965	Marlee Matlin	1/14/1875	Albert Schweitzer
11/21/1965	Bjork Gudmundsdottir	1/19/1879	W. C. Fields
11/30/1965	Ben Stiller	8/17/1892	Mae West
4/9/1966	Cynthia Nixon	11/23/1892	Erté
11/2/1966	David Schwimmer	4/20/1893	Joan Miro
2/10/1967	Laura Dern	6/9/1893	Cole Porter

2/3/1894	Norman Rockwell	1/8/1935	Elvis Presley
1/20/1896	George Burns	2/16/1935	Sonny Bono
7/9/1901	Barbara Cartland	3/15/1935	Judd Hirsch
2/4/1902	Charles Lindbergh	3/5/1936	Dean Stockwell
3/11/1903	Lawrence Welk	5/3/1936	Engelbert Humperdinck
5/16/1905	Henry Fonda	6/1/1937	Morgan Freeman
12/25/1907	Cab Calloway	8/8/1937	Dustin Hoffman
5/30/1909	Benny Goodman	4/1/1939	Ali McGraw
6/20/1909	Errol Flynn	1/21/1940	Jack Nicklaus
3/3/1911	Jean Harlow	3/10/1940	Chuck Norris
5/18/1912	Perry Como	6/7/1940	Tom Jones
5/27/1912	Sam Snead	6/7/1940	Gwendolyn Brooks
8/15/1912	Julia Child	12/1/1940	Richard Pryor
10/31/1912	Dale Evans	3/18/1941	Wilson Pickett
11/2/1913	Burt Lancaster	12/9/1941	Beau Bridges
4/7/1915	Billie Holiday	2/9/1942	Carol King
2/26/1916	Jackie Gleason	3/26/1942	Erica Jong
4/15/1916	Alfred Bloomingdale	7/13/1942	Harrison Ford
2/11/1922	Leslie Nielsen	9/29/1942	Madeline Kahn
4/27/1922	Jack Klugman	10/1/1942	Jim Croce
11/11/1922	Kurt Vonnegut	11/18/1942	Linda Evans
4/16/1924	Henry Mancini	11/27/1942	Jimi Hendrix
10/1/1924	Pres. Jimmy Carter	5/5/1943	Michael Palin
2/8/1925	Jack Lemmon	11/17/1943	Lauren Hutton
10/27/1925	Warren Christopher	1/17/1944	Joe Frazier
3/6/1926	Alan Greenspan	1/26/1944	Angela Davis
1/16/1927	Eartha Kitt	3/15/1944	Sly Stone
6/3/1926	Allen Ginsberg	2/24/1945	Barry Bostwick
6/28/1928	Mel Brooks	2/14/1946	Gregory Hines
1/4/1930	Don Shula	5/20/1946	Cher
9/23/1930	Ray Charles	6/19/1946	Gena Rowlands
11/30/1930	G. Gordon Liddy	2/4/1947	Dan Quayle
11/10/1932	Roy Scheider	4/2/1947	Emmylou Harris
2/18/1933	Yoko Ono	9/6/1947	Jane Curtin
4/7/1933	Wayne Rogers	3/20/1948	Bobby Orr
11/26/1933	Robert Goulet	9/14/1948	Nell Carter
3/7/1934	Willard Scott	8/23/1949	Shelly Long
3/25/1934	Gloria Steinem	8/23/1949	Rick Springfield
4/24/1934	Shirley MacClaine	11/29/1949	Gary Shandling
7/12/1934	Van Cliburn	1/29/1950	Ann Jillian
9/28/1934	Bridgett Bardot	2/10/1950	Mark Spitz

9/21/1950	Bill Murray	12/22/1973	Heather Donahue
11/28/1950	Ed Harris	12/29/1975	Shawn Hatosy
3/17/1951	Kurt Russell	4/18/1976	Melissa Joan Hart
8/30/1951	Timothy Bottoms	8/28/1980	Carly Pope
7/21/1952	Robin Williams	4/30/1982	Kristin Dunst
7/11/1953	Leon Spinks	6/10/1982	Leelee Sobieski
8/18/1954	Patrick Swayze		
10/7/1954	Corbin Bernsen		
3/20/1957	Spike Lee		
3/10/1958	Sharon Stone		
6/7/1958	Prince (Roger Nelson)		
3/18/1959	Irene Cara		
11/28/1959	Judd Nelson		
5/6/1960	Roma Downey		
9/29/1960	John Paxson		
1/17/1962	Jim Carrey		
2/7/1962	Garth Brooks		
7/19/1963	Anthony Edwards		
8/9/1963	Whitney Houston		
12/23/1963	Jim Harbaugh		
7/9/1964	Courtney Love		
9/16/1964	Molly Shannon		
12/4/1964	Marisa Tomei		
1/5/1965	Vinnie Jones		
6/8/1966	Julianna Margulies		
1/12/1967	Vendela		
1/2/1968	Cuba Gooding, Jr.		
1/1/1969	Verne Troyer		
4/7/1969	Jack Black		
4/25/1969	Renee Zellweger		
6/14/1969	Steffi Graf		
6/30/1971	Monica Potter		
9/9/1971	Goran Visnjic		
10/17/1971	Christopher Kirkpatrick		
5/12/1972	Christina Campbell		
7/1/1972	Claire Fonlani		
11/6/1972	Thandie Newton		
11/6/1972	Rebecca Romijn-Stamos		
9/7/1973	Shannon Elizabeth (Fadel)		
9/25/1973	Bridgette Wilson		
12/4/1973	Tyra Banks		

Appendix

WIZARD'S STAR WORKSHEET

Wizard's Star

Name:_____

Birth Date: _____

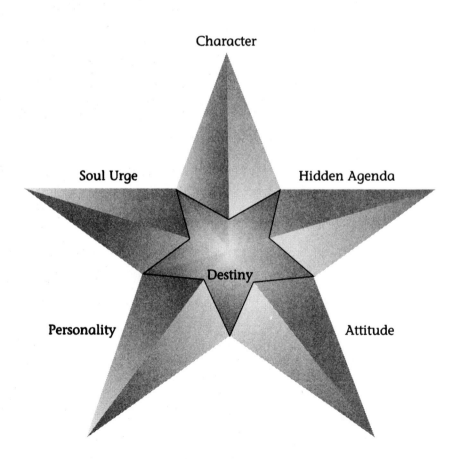

NUMEROLOGY WORKSHEETS

CALCULATE YOUR DESTINY NUMBER

Add Your Month, Day, and Year of birth together and reduce to a single digit (or a Master number – 11 or 22):

Vertical Method:

_____ + _____ + _____ = _____
  Month   Day   Year   Compound

Then continue adding any compound numbers (unless they reduce to the 11 or 22) together until you have a single digit:

_____ + _____ = _____   _____ + _____ = _____

Horizontal Method:

Month   _____
             +
Day   _____
             +
Year   _____

Equals   _____

Add together the remaining four numbers until you have a single digit or a Master number:

_____ + _____ + _____ + _____ = _____

Continue reducing, if necessary: _____ + _____ = _____

_____ + _____ = _____

My Destiny Number is: _____

Regardless of which way you add (vertical or horizontal), you should arrive at the same single digit number. However, if you may arrive at the single digit of 2 or 4 using one method and the 11 or 22 using the other method, it is suggested that you read the definitions for each number to determine which definition is most like you.

DETERMINE YOUR PERSONALITY NUMBER

Your Personality number is determined by the day of the month you were born. For example, if you were born on the 15th of any month, your Personality number is the number 15/6 (1 + 5 = 6).

My Personality Number is: _____

DETERMINE YOUR ATTITUDE NUMBER

Your Attitude number is derived from adding your month of birth to your day of birth and reducing that number to a single digit.

Example: If you were born on December 24th, you would add 12 (December) to 24 which equals 36 and then add 3 + 6, which equals 9. Your Attitude number is 9.

Your Attitude Number is: _____

DETERMINE YOUR CHARACTER NUMBER

Your Character number is derived from adding all the numbers associated with your full name from birth together and reducing the remainder to a single digit.

Refer to the alphabet chart on page 11 and/or Chapter 6 to determine the numbers associated with your name and how to add them together and continue to reduce the compound numbers until you have either a Master number or a single digit.

First Name: __ __ __ __ __ __ __ __ __ __ = __, __ + __ = ____

Middle Name: __ __ __ __ __ __ __ __ __ __ = __, __ + __ = ____
2ND
Middle Name: __ __ __ __ __ __ __ __ __ = __, __ + __ = ____

Last Name: __ __ __ __ __ __ __ __ __ = __, __ + __ = ____

My Character Number is: _____

DETERMINE YOUR SOUL URGE NUMBER

This number is derived from adding together all the numbers associated with the VOWELS in your name from birth. Refer to Chapter 6 for the example of how to calculate the Soul Urge number and follow the same addition process as you did to determine your Character number.

VOWELS ONLY:

First Name: __ __ __ __ __ __ __ __ __ __ = __, __ + __ = ____

Middle Name: __ __ __ __ __ __ __ __ __ __ = __, __ + __ = ____
2ND
Middle Name: __ __ __ __ __ __ __ __ __ = __, __ + __ = ____

Last Name: __ __ __ __ __ __ __ __ __ = __, __ + __ = ____

My Soul Urge Number is: _____

DETERMINE YOUR HIDDEN AGENDA NUMBER

This number is derived from adding together all the numbers associated with the CONSONANTS in your name from birth. Refer to Chapter 6 for the example of how to calculate the Hidden Agenda and follow the same addition process as you did to determine your Character and Soul Urge numbers.

CONSONANTS ONLY:

First Name: _ _ _ _ _ _ _ _ _ _ = __, __ + __ = ___

Middle Name: _ _ _ _ _ _ _ _ _ _ = __, __ + __ = ___
2ND
Middle Name: _ _ _ _ _ _ _ _ _ _ = __, __ + __ = ___

Last Name: _ _ _ _ _ _ _ _ _ _ = __, __ + __ = ___

My Hidden Agenda Number is: _____

DETERMINE YOUR DIVINE PURPOSE NUMBER

Add your Destiny number to your Character Number and reduce to a single digit.

My Purpose Number is: _____

DETERMINE YOUR PERSONAL YEAR

Add your Month of birth to your Day of birth. Then, add that number to the Universal Year number (see page 101), and reduce it down until it is either a Master number (11 or 22) or a single digit (1 through 9).

Example: Month and Day of Birth: December 24. Add 12 (December) to 24, which equals 36. Then, add 36 to 3 (the Universal Year number for 2001), which equals 39. Add 3 + 9 which equals 12. Then, add 1 + 2 which equals 3. The Personal Year for 2001 for someone born on December 21 is 3.

____ + ____ = ____   ____ + ____ = ____   ____ + ____ = ____

My Personal Year Number is: _____

DETERMINE YOUR PERSONAL MONTH

Add your Personal Year number to the current month number and reduce to a single digit.

____ + ____ = ____   ____ + ____ = ____   ____ + ____ = ____

My Personal Month Number is: _____

DETERMINE YOUR PERSONAL DAY

Add your Personal Month number to the current day of the month, and reduce to a single digit.

____ + ____ = ____   ____ + ____ = ____   ____ + ____ = ____

My Personal Day Number is: _____